GCSE
SOCIAL AND ECONOMIC
HISTORY

Ed Rayner
Ron Stapley

COURSEWORK
GUIDES

Longman

EDITORS' PREFACE

The introduction of GCSE created many challenges for both teachers and pupils, not least the idea that, for most subjects, the grade awarded should be based not only on examination performance but also on the assessment of certain pieces of coursework. Whilst this concept has been welcomed in most educational circles as relieving some or all of the stress associated with examinations, it is also recognised as imposing other sorts of pressures on pupils. To achieve good results, it is necessary to keep up to date, be organised, and most importantly, maintain an appropriate standard *from the beginning of the course*.

Longman Coursework Guides have been written by experienced examiners to give GCSE candidates help with such tasks as choosing, researching and writing up topics. In addition, the authors give many examples of (and comments upon) typical student assignments.

We believe that the books will stimulate as well as instruct, and will enable students to produce coursework which will truly reflect the level of commitment and effort which the GCSE demands.

Geoff Black and Stuart Wall

ACKNOWLEDGEMENTS

The authors are grateful to the Hulton Picture Company, the Greater London Record Office and History Library, the Royal Photographic Society and the Sutcliffe Gallery for permission to reproduce photographs.

LONGMAN COURSEWORK GUIDES

SERIES EDITORS
Geoff Black and Stuart Wall

TITLES AVAILABLE
Art and Design
Biology
Business Studies
CDT: Design and Realisation
Chemistry
Computer Studies
Economics
English
English Literature
Geography
Mathematics
Physics
Religious Studies
Science
Social and Economic History
World History

Longman Group UK Limited,
Longman House, Burnt Mill, Harlow,
Essex CM20 2JE, England
and Associated Companies throughout the world.

© Longman Group UK Limited 1989
All rights reserved; no part of this publication
may be reproduced, stored in a retrieval system,
or transmitted in any form or by any means, electronic,
mechanical, photocopying, recording, or otherwise,
without the prior written permission of the Publishers.

First published 1989

British Library Cataloguing in Publication Data

Rayner, E.G. (Edgar Geoffrey), 1927
  Social and economic history. – (Longman GCSE
  coursework guides)
  1. England. Secondary schools. Curriculum subjects:
  History. G.C.S.E. examinations
  I. Title   II. Stapley, R.F. (Ronald Frank), 1927
  907'.6

ISBN 0-582-05185-1

Produced by The Pen and Ink Book Company,
Huntingdon, Cambridgeshire

Set in 10/11pt Century Old Style

Printed and bound in Great Britain by
William Clowes Limited, Beccles and London

CONTENTS

	EDITORS' PREFACE	ii
	ACKNOWLEDGEMENTS	ii
CHAPTER 1	Nature and Importance of Coursework	1
	UNIT 1 INTRODUCTION	1
	UNIT 2 THE ROLE OF COURSEWORK	1
	UNIT 3 SKILLS TO BE TESTED BY COURSEWORK	3
	3.1 Knowledge-based skills	3
	3.2 Conceptual understanding	4
	3.3 Empathy	5
	3.4 Using sources	8
	UNIT 4 COURSEWORK REQUIREMENTS OF THE EXAM GROUPS	10
	4.1 London and East Anglian Group (LEAG)	10
	4.2 Midland Examining Group (MEG)	11
	4.3 Northern Examining Association (NEA)	12
	4.4 Northern Ireland Schools Examinations Council: Modular (NISEC)	12
	4.5 Southern Examining Group (SEG)	13
	4.6 Welsh Joint Education Committee: Modular (WJEC)	14
	UNIT 5 COURSEWORK MANAGEMENT	14
	5.1 Planning your work	14
	5.2 Enjoying your work	14
CHAPTER 2	Researching a Topic	16
	UNIT 1 CHOOSING A TOPIC AND A TITLE	16
	1.1 Documentary assignments	16
	1.2 Empathetic assignments	18
	1.3 Evaluation or Assessment assignments	19
	UNIT 2 SOURCES OF INFORMATION	22
	2.1 Libraries	22
	2.2 Archive sources	25
	2.3 Museums	26
	2.4 Historical fieldwork	27
	2.5 History games and computer programs	28
	UNIT 3 METHODS FOR EXTRACTING INFORMATION	29
	3.1 Books and Newspapers	29
	3.2 TV, sound broadcast and film	30
	3.3 Visits and field trips	30
	3.4 Documentary sources	30
CHAPTER 3	Using Statistics and Evidence Material	34
	UNIT 1 MAPS AND ILLUSTRATIONS	34
	1.1 Maps	34

		1.2 Illustrations	38
	UNIT 2	THE USE OF STATISTICAL MATERIAL	42
		2.1 Statistical tables	42
		2.2 Statistical diagrams	43
		2.3 Graphs	47
	UNIT 3	COMMON PROBLEMS WITH STATISTICS	49
		3.1 Misleading averages	49
		3.2 Misleading bar charts	50
		3.3 Misleading graphs	50
		3.4 Misleading picture diagrams	51
		3.5 Incomplete evidence	52
		3.6 English, British and UK statistics	52
		3.7 Money prices and real prices	53
		3.8 Old and new currencies	54
		3.9 Indices	55
		3.10 Visible and invisible trade	56
CHAPTER 4	Preparing and presenting a Coursework assignment		58
	UNIT 1	STUDY ON INDUSTRIAL CHANGE	58
		1.1 Planning	58
		1.2 Preparation	59
		1.3 Completing the writing	61
		1.4 Examiner's mark scheme	64
	UNIT 2	STUDY USING DOCUMENTARY SOURCES	64
		2.1 Planning and preparation	66
		2.2 Completing the writing	66
		2.3 Examiner's mark scheme	68
CHAPTER 5	Examples of Students' Coursework		69
	UNIT 1	INDUSTRIAL DEVELOPMENTS SINCE 1870	69
	UNIT 2	THE GENERAL STRIKE: A WORKING CLASS REVOLUTION?	71
	UNIT 3	RAILWAY BUILDING	73
	UNIT 4	WOMEN IN SOCIETY, 1890–1940	76
	UNIT 5	WAR AND SOCIAL AND ECONOMIC CHANGE	79
	UNIT 6	NINETEENTH-CENTURY RAILWAYS	82
	UNIT 7	CHILD LABOUR IN THE NINETEENTH CENTURY	85
	UNIT 8	EMIGRATION IN THE NINETEENTH CENTURY	88

NATURE AND IMPORTANCE OF COURSEWORK

UNIT 1 INTRODUCTION

How to use this book

This is meant to be a 'user-friendly' sort of book. Coming to it at the age of fourteen or fifteen, at the outset of your GCSE History course, you may feel dismayed by its length and complexity, and even hesitant about the big task of starting to plough your way through it. However we hope that this short introduction will take away any such fears.

Though each section follows on from the one before, you do not by any means have to read the *whole* of the book at once. Using the chapter titles and the Contents you can in fact read it in any order, turning at once to the part of it that you wish to consult and concentrating on that part alone for the time being.

Summary of the book

Chapter 1 deals first of all with the part which coursework plays in the GCSE scheme of examining, telling you what coursework is for and showing the ways in which it is meant to be helpful. The chapter then goes on to introduce you to the idea of historical *skills*, on which the assessment is largely based. Knowledge-based skills are dealt with first, and key concepts such as cause and consequence, continuity and change, and similarity and difference are introduced. Then the chapter introduces you to the notion of *empathy*, and brings in the more complex notion of *differentiated empathy*. Source-based skills are the next to be discussed. Different kinds of sources are mentioned, and there is some discussion of *primary* and of *secondary* sources. Then the skills associated with the use of sources are discussed. Unit 4 of this chapter lists the various coursework requirements of different GCSE groups, while Unit 5 gives you a few tips on the proper management of your coursework activities.

Chapter 2 sets out the method of *researching* a historical topic for a coursework assignment. It discusses different kinds of assignment, and goes on to make quite detailed comments on your likely sources of information. You may be in a position where you do not need all of this, especially if your teacher has provided the sources for you; but you may find it interesting, nevertheless, if you want to hunt out material for yourself. The chapter concludes by making some recommendations on your best methods of investigation.

Chapter 3 deals with ways in which you can make the *best use of your material*, and deals with maps, photographs, cartoons, etc. It also deals at some length with things directly relating to the social and economic side of this work – tables, diagrams, graphs and so on. The chapter ends with a 'trouble-shooting' Unit, alerting you to some problems in the handling of social and economic material, and dealing with the more difficult economic formulae.

The last two chapters deal with the actual *preparation* and *presentation* of coursework assignments. Chapter 4 gives detailed guidance on how this can be done, and Chapter 5 contains a long list of worked examples of coursework assignments, each of them with examiner comments. This is a long chapter, and you may not need all of it; but on the other hand the examples themselves may prove quite interesting. Study as many of them as you like at whatever time you like.

UNIT 2 THE ROLE OF COURSEWORK

All the Social and Economic History syllabuses offered by the various GCSE Groups contain a coursework element. This forms a very important part of the task before you when you start the subject. The coursework is marked by your teacher, and reviewed afterwards by other teachers and examiners appointed by the Examining Group for which you have been entered. Together they decide the final mark that is to be awarded. It is this mark – counting up to 30% of the overall total – which goes towards deciding your final grade in the whole examination process. The aim of this book is to help you with the *preparation* and the *presentation* of your coursework. It gives details of coursework *objectives*, the *nature* of coursework assignments, the *relationship* between the different types of coursework and the coursework objectives, and *practical advice* on the best ways of fulfilling coursework requirements.

You will, of course, be required to submit coursework not solely in Social and Economic History, but in other subjects as well. This is why, from the beginning, you have to learn to *plan* your time so that proper attention is paid to every subject, and not just to the few which you prefer. If you let your coursework pile up, you will find yourself getting into increasing difficulties.

> **Good coursework gets you a better grade**

The inclusion of coursework in the examination is meant not as a tiresome extra, but as a *bonus*. What it means, in effect, is that a quarter of the marks, or more, are being awarded to you without the pressure of an examination and as the result of your own individual efforts. Under the old examination system everything depended on a two-and-a-half hour examination on a single day at the end of the course. Even for able students, such an arrangement created uncertainty and worry. Have you chosen the right topics to revise? Have you learnt the work sufficiently thoroughly? Are you going to get the right questions on the paper? Are you going to be able to get down all you know in the time allowed? Even students who have worked well throughout the two-year course have been known to turn in a disappointing performance on the day, especially if they are a bit off-colour, or feel unduly nervous about their chances. With coursework, on the other hand, a lot of this pressure is relieved. You can work at your own pace, take as long as you like, put in as much preparation as you need, and employ the assistance of all the books available to you. The nightmare of having to rely solely on your memory, with the clock ticking relentlessly in the background, is no longer so frightening. Of course, written examinations have not been abandoned altogether. In fact, there are usually *two* papers, whereas before there was only one. Each paper tests different things: your ability to produce short answers; your ability to write an essay answer; your ability to employ evidence and to process data; and so forth. But the inclusion of a sizeable coursework element enables credit to be given for good work *throughout the course*, and not merely on examination day. This gives you a clear chance, if you choose to employ it, to improve your performance in the whole examination.

As part of the assessment process, you will be tackling written assignments from the early part of your course in the fourth year, and these assignments will count towards the final grading as much as the later ones. Hence it is important that, from early on in the course, you should know what you are supposed to be doing.

There are various ways of *presenting* coursework in the subject. Your teacher will be familiar with the rules and will be able to advise you if you have some ideas of your own. The rules of most Exam Groups have nothing to stop you from building a model, making a tape-recording or producing a video, or making a report on a visit to some site of interest in industrial archaeology. The Groups, of course, have to insist that the work is individual work if they are to make an individual assessment; hence they cannot accept anything that results from teamwork. The fact remains, however, that most coursework assignments will take the form of *written work*, even if this work is supported by photographs, drawings or tape-recordings.

You should not assume, as some students and many parents do, that coursework means *projects*. At one time projects formed the main part of the coursework diet, frequently involving lengthy and detailed research, leading to marathon writing efforts approaching book size in final form. Experience revealed that such projects took up too much time, and often resulted in much mindless copying from the sources on which they were based. The prospect of this kind of enterprise carried on across the range of six or seven subjects would be too frightening to contemplate. Mercifully, this is not the case. Coursework in subjects is now asking for something more *manageable*, and *arising directly* from the course itself. Some Groups, it is true, allow you to present one piece of written work of up to 4500 words – something very like a project; but many allow you to split it into two, or more, shorter pieces of work, sometimes related to a common theme. These then need be only of essay length, or even shorter. The Southern Examining Group asks for two essays, neither to exceed 1000 words; the Northern Examining Association from four to six written assignments, not exceeding an overall total of 6000 words. Groups generally agree that falling below the minimum number of words may result in candidates being penalized, but work in excess of the maximum is not likely to be penalized unless it exceeds the maximum by a substantial margin.

Much of the coursework expected will consist of work done in class, and will take the form of the best work which a candidate submits during the course. The assignments will have to cover the skills specified in the Group regulations, and these will be familiar to the teachers who set the work over the two years in which the subject is being prepared.

It is now the practice of most Groups to ask for coursework proposals to be submitted in advance, so as to avoid students wasting time on titles which do not satisfactorily meet their requirements. Hence the *titles* of the assignments, their *subject content*, and some detail on *how marks will be awarded* all have to be agreed before any coursework can usefully be attempted. This is to make sure that the coursework set is of a suitable standard to meet the

❝ Coursework proposals in advance ❞

Group's requirements. It is possible that a teacher, unfamiliar with the regulations, or working in isolation from other teachers, may set coursework which fails to test some of the required skills. The Group's regulations are meant to prevent this mishap. All teachers are required to think out their proposals, and then to submit them to a body of expert examiners employed by the Group for the purpose. The Northern Examining Association is one of those for whom advanced submission of coursework proposals is now compulsory, and it requires notification of coursework details by 15 February of the first year of the two-year course. This makes it difficult for candidates to devise their own coursework proposals – indeed, if you want to do so, you will have to talk over your own proposals with your teacher very early and possibly within the first term of starting on your course.

UNIT 3 SKILLS TO BE TESTED BY COURSEWORK

All the Examining Groups specify in detail the *historical skills* which they intend shall be tested in the coursework, and lay down the proportions in which the marks are to be *allocated* to these various skills. The proportions vary from one Group to another. Most of them ask for *all four* skills (see below) to be tested. The Southern Examining Group, however, concentrates chiefly on two of these skills – the skill of seeing the past from the point of view of those who lived in it (a skill known as *empathy*), and the skill of handling a wide variety of historical sources.

Though each Group tends to analyse these abilities or skills rather differently, there are basically *four* of them that the coursework (and the written examination) will be trying to test and to measure. These abilities are called the *assessment objectives* of the coursework part of the examination.

3.1 Knowledge-based skills

❝ Skill 1 ❞

The first objective is stated by the National Criteria to be the ability 'to recall, evaluate and select knowledge relevant to the context and to deploy it in a clear and coherent form.' This would seem to be an objective of overriding importance in a subject like History, and at least one of the Groups acknowledges this by awarding a double weighting to this skill. At the same time, it should be admitted that there are a good many teachers who believe that the skill of 'recall' is one that is best measured in examination conditions rather than in coursework assignments, and these people dwell less heavily on it as a prime factor, taking the view that if candidates are surrounded by all their textbooks and other materials (as they are likely to be in coursework) any deficiencies in 'recall' can speedily be remedied.

However, 'recall' is not the *only* skill that derives from factual knowledge. If you look at the criterion set out above a second time, you will see there is more to it than simply 'recall'. You have to be able to *evaluate* information, and to *select* it as useful in the context of the work you are doing; and then you have to be able to set it out in a *clear* and *coherent* form. Candidates do not always find these tasks easy to perform, even though they are surrounded by the factual material.

EVALUATION

Evaluation involves distinguishing the more important from the less important, and the relevant from the irrelevant. It also means that you have to be able to distinguish bias from impartiality, to detect inconsistencies and gaps, and to comment intelligently on the *authenticity*, the *reliability* and the *validity* of the evidence before you. More information on such matters is to be found in Chapter 2 of this book, but for the time being it should be said that evaluation is by no means an easy matter. Indeed, the greater the mass of the historical material, the more difficult it often seems to become. The unsuspecting GCSE candidate can soon find himself or herself overwhelmed by historical information and hardly knowing where to begin to evaluate it.

SELECTION

Selection is a skill often very seriously underrated by GCSE candidates. Some of them even seem to think that to select at all is a regrettable sign of laziness, since it is obviously better to include everything, and then there can be no doubt about the outcome. By substituting thoroughness for intelligence they hope to conceal the fact that they are not willing to back their judgment and make a choice. A moment's thought will show you how wrong this is. No one can possibly set out all the facts, partly because no one knows what all the facts are, and because, *even if they did*, limitations of space and energy would prevent them using all of them. Indeed, the converse is true. A better case is often made by a single point skilfully chosen than by a mass of material undiscriminatingly employed.

CLARITY

Clarity is the skill by which one thing is defined and distinguished from another; it is the skill of *analysis*. You are said to analyse things when you take them apart into their component elements in order to see what makes them what they are. You are not required to have any deep knowledge of chemistry to distinguish between iron and steel when you are writing about the metal industries, but you have to use the two terms consistently, to distinguish between them and to write about them in such a way that an examiner in economic history will be able to follow you. And the same applies to arguments as to individual terms; it is very easy to *know* what you mean, but to be incapable of *expressing* it clearly.

COHERENCE

Coherence is the skill by which ideas are put together and combined into an effective whole; it is the skill of *synthesis*. When you explain the connection between deflation, unemployment and industrial recession, you will have to show that you understand how these things *interrelate*, i.e. how they are connected with each other. When, in your written work, you are setting out an argument to do with these things, you must not only use the terms clearly, but you must state your argument coherently, by showing how one step sensibly leads to the next.

You will see, therefore, that there is much more to this assessment objective than recall alone. That is why knowledge-based assignments continue to have their proper place in the scheme of assessment.

3.2 Conceptual understanding

The second assessment objective is 'the ability to make use of and to understand the concepts of cause and consequence, continuity and change, similarity and difference.' These are agreed to be amongst the *concepts* which students of social and economic history – and, indeed *all* history – should be able to manage. These three sets of opposites are essential to a good understanding of the subject.

CAUSE AND CONSEQUENCE

This pair is intended to cover relationships brought about by *cause*, i.e. circumstances which lead to the bringing about of an event, and *effect*, i.e. circumstances resulting from an event.

The first deals with *Why?* questions and is concerned with *reasons*. Thus a question of this sort might enquire: 'Why was it thought necessary to introduce the Poor Law Amendment Act in 1834?'

The second concerns itself with *results*. A question of this sort might ask: 'What were the effects of the First World War on British industry and trade?' You may find that you already have in your history notes a number of instances where the causes, or the results, of an event are listed; and these are clearly things which you may be expected to learn in the course of your studies. But you also have to be able to work them out, and to understand them for yourself. Both causes and results – though perhaps separately numbered in your notes as individual points – are not to be seen in isolation. They usually work together and operate on each other, producing what is sometimes called 'a complex *web* of cause and effect.'

CONTINUITY AND CHANGE

This pair deals with the nature of historical *change* and the *pace* of this change. From your history you will see that some things change, whilst others remain the same. Value judgments may attach to this change, in which case you will use words such as 'develop', 'grow' or 'mature', or alternatively 'alter' or 'deteriorate'. The things that are unchanging will continue as a background to this more rapid movement; and these unchanging things will either not change at all, or else will change much more slowly. The difference is one between *revolution* and *evolution*. Thus you ought to be able to see that a particular technical innovation may have brought about a revolution in an individual industry; but overall the pace of change in industry is more gradual, and is more akin to evolution than to revolution. The word 'progress' is used of changes of which you approve; a change that is thought to be regrettable is never referred to as progress.

SIMILARITY AND DIFFERENCE

You will see that the word 'difference' has already been used in the previous paragraph in a way that is quite self-explanatory; however, history students are not only looking for differences, but for similarities too. For example, you have to be able to point out the *similarities* in the motives of those in the nineteenth century who tried to reduce government intervention in trade by getting rid of tariffs, and the *differences* in the provisions of individual factory acts, all of which shared the same objective of protecting female workers and young people.

One of the things which shows a highly-developed understanding on the part of the student is the ability to make a *comparison*, and possibly an original one. The ability to compare, for example, the motives of the two pressure groups – one of which wished to reduce state intervention and the other of which wished to increase it – will throw up features of British nineteenth-century social and economic history which deserve further study. Further, your ability as a history student to 'compare and contrast' (that phrase once so beloved of examiners!) shows historical understanding of a high order.

Conceptual abilities will often be tested in *structured essays* (i.e in essays consisting of two or more sections dealing with different aspects of the subject) as included in the examination paper. But some coursework assignments could also be slanted towards this same objective. Thus an assignment which required a candidate to

> use the given source materials and secondary sources of your own choice to compare the effects of the Depression of the 1930s in a) Gateshead and b) Luton

would be testing partly objective 1 for the *selection and arrangement* of material, and objective 2 for the *comparison*, with the similarities and differences being highlighted.

Such an assignment would obviously require suitable sources relating to the two towns to be chosen by the teacher and made available for study, but it may be possible for *you* to find suitable documents yourself, and even perhaps persuade your teacher to adapt the coursework so as to include them. This may not be easy, since teachers generally have better access to documents than students do; but if you are keen to add your own personal touch, and if the materials are within your reach, you may be able to make your own contribution to the work. Remember that in choosing your own documents, the danger is often that you will use too many rather than too few. Remember what was said above about *selection*: a limited number of relevant documents that you can handle well, and which can most effectively make the points you would wish to mention, will be of much more value than a large number of documents of less relevance which you handle less convincingly.

3.3 Empathy

Skill 3

The third assessment objective is referred to as *empathy*, and involves the ability to look at people, events and issues in the past *as the people in the past would have looked at them*. This means that students will be expected to comment on history from the point of view of someone who was a contemporary of the subject under discussion. To do this well, you will be expected to show that people in the past had *their own views* of what was happening, and that the problems of the past were capable of being looked at *in different ways* by the people of the time. This imaginative transference is one of the more controversial aspects of History examining in the GCSE.

The present view is that there are broadly three levels of attainment in empathy:

Level 1: the recognition that people in the past had feelings and emotions, together with the unthinking assumption that such people had the ideas and feelings of the people of the 1980s, i.e. the mistaken view that ideas and feelings do not change over a period of time.

Level 2: the knowledge that people in the past had feelings *appropriate for that time period*, but with the mistaken assumption that *everyone felt the same* at the time. It would be a mistake, for example, for students to suggest that all the supporters of the Chartist movement were equally hostile to the Anti-Corn-Law League in the first half of the 1840s.

Level 3: The recognition that people thought *independently* and *differently* about the problems of the period, and that there were all sorts of different opinions current at that time, just as there are at present. Thus different individual employers had varying views about the new trade unions in the mid-nineteenth century, some of them thinking that they threatened revolution, whilst others thought of them as a good step towards securing the goodwill and the co-operation of the work-force.

Empathy work cannot be conducted in a vacuum. It requires detailed *historical knowledge* to make it convincing and realistic. You cannot, after all, be reasonably expected to put yourself into the shoes of someone you know nothing about. To write of the lives of slum-dwellers in Victorian times calls for more than conventional expressions of feelings about hunger, dirt and poverty; you must have a good knowledge of the conditions of the lower classes at that time.

As soon as you mention that the lift in your block of council flats is out of commission, or that it is difficult for your aged mother to leave the building to collect her old-age pension, you give yourself away. What you say has to ring true, and the emotions you express have to be appropriate to the period you are dealing with.

At present, GCSE Groups are moving away from including empathy questions in the written examination, and now prefer to confine empathy to coursework, where perhaps it operates less artificially. In coursework, it can score up to half the marks (usually 30%) available. It is therefore important to get it right. You must not think you can bluff your way through, or that by a few technical tricks you can fool the examiner into thinking you have mastered the period; you have undoubtedly to know what you are writing about. In particular you need to emphasise the *variety* of opinions held by people in the past, and to avoid the mistake of believing that people then thought exactly as people think at present. You must not assume that all working people supported the General Strike of 1926, and supported it for the same reasons. The fact is that many opposed it, and those who supported it did so for a whole variety of different reasons. To assume that the workers responded automatically with support for the views of A. J. Cook ('Not a penny off the pay, not a minute on the day') would be a travesty of the actual situation at the time.

The type of empathy exercise currently in use with the GCSE Groups ought to allow scope for showing various shades of opinion.

> How did Conservative cabinet ministers react to the suggestions of the Royal Commission on Old Age Pensions in 1896 that the Government should consider the adoption of such a scheme?

Here, it would be foolish to image that all Conservative cabinet ministers took the same view. Some might take the view that all the schemes discussed were ruinously expensive and would impose insupportable burdens on British industry, whilst others might take the view that however desirable old-age pension schemes might be, it was unfortunate that the Royal Commission had not strongly recommended one of the schemes it had discussed. Some cabinet members, like Chamberlain, might think that old-age pensions were a way of showing Conservative concern for the problems of working-class people and a sure-fire way of winning electoral support for the party at the polls.

Some questions may focus on *one* person, but will be put in the form of a *problem* rather than in the form of role-play. You would not be asked, for example, as British Prime Minister in 1904, whether you supported Joseph Chamberlain's proposals for Tariff Reform, but you might be asked:

66 Differentiated empathy 99

> In 1904, the British Prime Minister, Balfour, was considering whether or not to offer tariff protection to British industry by adopting a system of duties on imports. Despite his commitment to policies of free trade, this was not an easy decision to make. Why was this?

Here, you are not pretending to be the Prime Minister, but you are expected to look at the question of tariff reform from his point of view. If you show why, despite the party's long-standing commitment to the doctrine of free trade, there were good reasons why Balfour should wish to protect British trade and industry by a system of tariffs, then you are on your way to a Level 3 mark. To the Prime Minister, the decline in British industrial leadership, and the growth of foreign industrial competition, were such that protective tariffs were essential if British prices and the levels of industrial employment were to be maintained. But the party had a popular, and long- standing, electoral commitment to free trade policies, and could not expect to win an election on the unpopular platform of protection, especially if this meant an increase in the price of food-stuffs for working-class voters. Your answer should show that you appreciate the difficulty in which the Prime Minister found himself, and that you understand the reasons for his coming to the eventual conclusion that he reached in 1905 – namely that he should stand by the political stance which his party had for so long adopted, and trust that the strength of British industry was such that its temporary difficulties could be overcome without recourse to a policy of trade tariffs.

This outline for an empathy assignment on British trade policies at the beginning of the twentieth century gives you, of course, only *basic ideas* to help you to reach Level 3. You would have to develop these ideas to the required length if you were to succeed in your assignment – anything from 800 to 1200 words. It is possible that you might be expected to produce such an assignment with the help of secondary sources *only*, e.g. text-books and other reference sources, but this is unlikely. You are more likely to be provided with several pieces of *primary* source material – letters, extracts from diaries, newspapers and parliamentary reports, photographs, cartoons etc. You will then be expected to build up your understanding of the period by use of these pieces of evidence. Sometimes, your exercise will be a combination of an empathy exercise with one dealing with the handling of documentary sources. If, however, you are provided with sources in an exercise testing empathy only, do not allow yourself to get side-tracked into a discussion dealing with the importance of the sources: stick to the main point of the assignment.

CHAPTER ONE SKILLS TO BE TESTED BY COURSEWORK

It is, of course, possible that you may be given a *role-play* exercise. Do not worry too much! There are ways in which you can cope with this problem. Consider, for example, this exercise given to a student:

> It is September 1931, and the National Government has just introduced the Public Assistance Committee to administer the 'Means Test'. As a member of the working classes, how do you react to these new proposals?

❝ Study this example ❞

The student offered this answer:

I became unemployed in 1930, when the shipyard in the north-east where I was working closed down because of lack of orders. I was deeply disappointed that Ramsay MacDonald's Labour Government at the time did so little to help me — especially since the Prime Minister's own constituency was so close to this area of heavy unemployment. But though many of my friends in the shipyard believed that he had sold out to the employers by buying off their political opposition, I could not help thinking that even his most whole-hearted support could not succeed in generating commercial orders for new ships where, in a time of mass industrial depression, none existed. They derided his efforts to bring a National Government into being in 1931, condemning it as a desperate effort to remain in office; but I and a number of my friends could perfectly understand the need for policies of national regeneration, and could see that sacrifices had to be made to bring this about. To regard the man who for so long had shown himself to be the honest friend of the working man as a careerist and a traitor seemed so unlikely as to invite the suspicion that it was inspired by those who wished the working-class movement no good.

But directly after the election in September which returned this National Government to office, MacDonald and his ministers moved against the unemployed. They imposed a cut of 10% in unemployment payments as part of an economy package and introduced a 'Means Test' on benefits. Having to stand in line at the Employment Exchange waiting for some hard-faced official to deal with you is bad enough, but the way these people pry into your affairs is even worse. My two children have got jobs of a sort — the girl works part-time as a ticket-clerk in the bus office, and the boy delivers newspapers after school and makes and sells bundles of firewood at week-ends to help his mother out with the bills. But they only earn a shilling or two between them, and I certainly don't expect it to be knocked off my benefits. My mate at the end of the street says they even came round to his house enquiring how much he paid for his new pair of boots, and suggested he couldn't be too poor if he had them new and not from the jumble sale. Mrs. Higgins, next door to him, had an even worse deal. She found that her benefit had been docked because one of the government snoopers had been round — reckoned that she was cohabiting with her lodger because she hung her knickers alongside his pants on the washing line. Yet some of them at the Working Men's Club actually approve of the Means Test — it's easier, I expect, if you are comfortably in work yourself! They say they don't see why a chap whose children are earning should expect the state to keep him. Some of the newspapers actually suggest that the unemployed are idle loafers, and could get a job if they stirred themselves. Middle-class people talk about what they call 'equality of sacrifice' and ask how it can be right for everybody else to make economies except the unemployed who are always whingeing for more dole. Sacrifice, by God! As if we haven't made enough sacrifices already, fighting in the war, without now having to humiliate ourselves to beg for a crust of bread!

Now we've got the Unemployment Assistance Board, and this is meant to be an improvement. 'Assistance' — that's a laugh! But they still use the Means Test, and the scales of support, when you can prove you really need it, are very meagre. A married man, like myself, with two children, gets 27 shillings and 3 pence a week. That's handsome to keep a family on! I'd like to spit in the eye of any middle-class person who says what a privilege it is for the unemployed to draw such generous benefits. Strange, though, how my wife doesn't agree with me. Perhaps she thinks she's the lady of the manor, or something — but she's always criticizing the unemployed as scroungers, and yet I'm unemployed myself. She says there isn't the money to go on supporting the people in idleness, and we ought to try to help ourselves more. She holds up old Chapman who used to be store-keeper at the iron works as some sort of example to me, because he clears houses now and has set himself up as a second-hand furniture salesman. Doesn't make for harmony in the home, all the arguments we have!

It's depressing, living in a depressed area, with men standing on street corners, the shops closing because shop-keepers can't make a living, and children with no future leaving school at fourteen to go straight on to the dole with their fathers. The trouble is we can't even afford to move where the work is — otherwise I'd be off tomorrow.

This exercise is about 900 words long, and is perhaps not quite long enough for the requirements of some Groups. But it has quite a lot of empathy, in spite of its *role-play* format. The technique is to make sure that the central figure who is telling you the story knows of plenty of other people – some of them in much the same position as himself – with whom he *disagrees*, thus showing the wide range of opinion necessary to reach Level 3. Here, we see someone who starts by defending the position of the National Government until he feels the pinch of the Means Test. Then he gets angry at the way he is treated; but others amongst his work-mates take a different view, and even his wife suggests he might try to go into business for himself instead of just drawing the dole. These are pointers towards a good Level 3. If you are given such an exercise you can tackle it in a similar way.

3.4 Using sources

❝ **Skill 4** ❞

The fourth assessment objective concerns itself with the handling of various kinds of *historical sources*. Some Groups, such as the SEG, devote half their coursework to this objective – as well as testing it in the examination itself – so that it is very important to be able to deal with all the various aspects of it. What follows is an introduction to a complicated subject; in later chapters you will see numerous examples of it in operation.

Firstly, you will be expected to distinguish between *primary* and *secondary* historical sources. Primary sources include photographs and artefacts (i.e. objects from the period), as well as written documents, suggesting first-hand evidence. These are produced at the time of the events they deal with, or very shortly afterwards. Secondary sources are produced afterwards, sometimes by people who were not involved in the events dealt with, and who indeed may not even have been alive at the time. Many biographies of historical persons, and most history textbooks, fall into this category. You will also be expected to *understand* and to *extract information* from the sources; to *interpret* the sources, and to distinguish between *fact, opinion* and *judgment*. You should be able to point out *deficiencies*, i.e. gaps in the evidence, and any *inconsistencies*, i.e. where the evidence is contradictory. Very importantly, you should also be able to detect *bias*. Where there are several pieces of evidence, you should be able to *compare* them, and to *reach conclusions* based on this comparison. None of this will come by light of nature, and you will have to have a good deal of practice before mastering the skills.

PRIMARY SOURCES

❝ **Primary sources** ❞

Primary sources are the building blocks of history. Here are some examples:
▶ a contemporary photograph of a hospital ward or of the interior of a prison can provide valuable information about what things were actually like;
▶ objects unearthed at the time of the excavation of a disused lime kiln can cast light on industrial conditions and processes in the early days of the Industrial Revolution;
▶ articles printed in a newspaper about railway or canal closures at the time of these events;
▶ documentary evidence produced by official records, or in the accounts of eye-witnesses to historical events such as Bleriot's first crossing of the Channel by air in 1909.

Newspapers date from the time of the events they describe, and although their evidence is not always first-hand, they are usually regarded as primary sources. This is because, being written at the time, they lack the benefit of hindsight, i.e. of being wise after the event. Written sources produced so long after the events they deal with that they can no longer be thought of as contemporary are regarded as *secondary sources*. This is true of all history textbooks.

Of course, we must not jump to the conclusion that because they are contemporary documents, primary sources are necessarily *more reliable* than secondary ones. Eye-witnesses may have particular reasons for misrepresenting what they have seen: they may be biased, or have a particular viewpoint to justify. They may have seen only part of the event that they claim to describe. They may even be lying. It is often easy to see this if two contemporary sources dealing with with the same events are compared. If you look at the evidence given by different witnesses to the Royal Commissioners on Factory Conditions in 1833 you will see heart-rending evidence given by little children on the kind of hours they worked, and the conditions they worked in; but the views of the employers were quite different, and it is hard to believe that both sides were talking about the same situation. The same is true of the conflicting evidence given to the Mines' Commissioners in 1843: young people with their tales of hardship, toil and brutality, and the mineowners' view of conditions in the collieries. Bearing in mind that there were lying workmen as well as truthful ones, and humane employers as well as cruel ones, you might be forgiven for thinking it almost impossible to get to the bottom of the situation.

It is important to remember that where you have only *one* primary source this may be just as one-sided as the obviously biased evidence referred to above. The fact that there is no other account to contradict the first does *not* mean that it is absolutely reliable and truthful. You may be unaware that your primary source is distorted, or has omitted or suppressed important facts, but your approach to a single, unsupported source should always take this possibility into account. Two sources taking the same view, of course, *corroborate* each other's testimony; but even here you must be sure that the information from the second does not derive from the first. If the two documents are suspiciously in cahoots with each other you would be justified in feeling doubtful about both of them. The trouble with history students is that they are often too gullible: if they see things in print, they are inclined to suppose they must certainly be true.

Your task is easier if your source uses the sort of language which clearly betrays its bias. As late as 1861 it was said of school-teachers:

None are too old, too poor, too ignorant, too feeble, too sickly, too unqualified in any and every way to regard themselves, and to be regarded by others, as unfit for school-keeping. Domestic servants out of place; discharged barmaids; vendors of toys and lollipops; keepers of small eating-houses or small lodging-houses; needle-women who take in plain or slop work, milliners, consumptive patients in an advanced stage, cripples almost bed-ridden, persons of at least doubtful temperance . . . such are some of the teachers, not in remote rural districts, but in the heart of London.

The fact that this is from an official government report *(The Report on the State of Popular Education in England (1861),* known from the name of its Chairman as the *Newcastle Report)* should not lead you to suppose that it is entirely impartial in its treatment of its subject. The authors of the Report clearly have their own axe to grind. Can you see what it is? They paint the supply of teachers in the blackest possible colours. They do this by employing weapons of *exaggeration,* in phrases like 'in any and every way', by sardonic humour, 'vendors of toys and lollipops', and by appealing to the popular prejudices of the time against 'consumptive' patients and against persons of 'doubtful temperance' (i.e. drunks). All this is somewhat less than the cool, dispassionate civil service language which we might feel entitled to expect from government reports.

Remember at the same time, though there may be an obvious bias in a source, this does not make it automatically valueless. Such a source as the one quoted above shows that enlightened opinion in 1861 was so outraged at teacher supply that it felt justified in being sarcastic about it. Though there was exaggeration in the way their ideas were expressed, the members of the enquiry had good reason to be dissatisfied with the situation, and there was every justification for the view that the most unsuitable people found employment as school teachers.

Sources which are biased may be unreliable for someone seeking the truth about what happened; but they may still be very useful to historians in showing the prejudices of their period. The suspicions of Anglicans that the Education Act of 1870 might be used against the established church; the feeling of Non-conformists that state help ought to be used to prevent their children from being brain-washed into the Church of England – even the apparently harmless statement by Joseph Chamberlain (himself a Non-conformist) to the effect that

In the present state of religious parties, no agreement as to a common theological instruction can be arrived at, therefore the new schools must be thoroughly non-sectarian.

show that all the opinions that were offered by contemporary commentators were coloured by religious conviction. Anglicans suspected that Non-conformists, having little money of their own to put into education, were keen to use state funds for spreading simple Bible teaching and so undermining the Anglican Catechism; Non-conformists feared that unless there was freedom of conscience, the Church would use its wealth and resources to instil Anglican beliefs into their children attending church schools; whilst commentators who were apparently neutral in the conflict put forward views which on closer inspection could be seen to favour one side or the other. What would you say, for example were the prejudices of a commentator who said the following in 1867?

I suppose now it will be absolutely necessary to educate our masters. I was before this opposed to centralization (in education); I am now ready to accept centralization... From the moment you entrust

CHAPTER ONE NATURE AND IMPORTANCE OF COURSEWORK

the masses with power their education becomes an imperative necessity. You have placed the government of this country in the hands of the masses, and you must therefore give them education.

Are these religious prejudices, or prejudices of some other sort? What kind of unspoken assumptions was he making when he said this? If you share these assumptions with the speaker, it may be difficult for you to recognize them as assumptions.

SECONDARY SOURCES

Secondary accounts written afterwards by historians are likely, of course, to offer a *more balanced* view. They are able to survey and sum the evidence on one side of the case, and balance it against that on the other side. Students are all too often ready to accept their verdict, and to regard it as a kind of higher truth. But you must remember that what you are being offered is in the last analysis no more than the opinion of the historian who has studied the period. His view may be prejudiced by factors so deeply buried that even the author does not recognize them for what they are. A lifelong supporter of the labour movement may regard Robert Owen as the 'father of socialism', however much the evidence may point to his being a humanitarian entrepreneur of individualist convictions. The production of mere evidence is hardly enough to upset this settled view. Curiously, the opposite may also sometimes be the case. Some supporters of socialism may be so anxious to do justice to their opponents that they lean over backwards to be fair to them, and perhaps finish by making bigger claims for conservatism than they would if they had been conservatives themselves. But once you have recognized the prejudices of the authors of secondary sources you are halfway to compensating for it in your own mind. The important thing is that you should not regard secondary sources as being disinterested and thoroughly impartial – they almost certainly are not.

Extended examples of the use of historical sources in coursework are to be found in Chapters 4 and 5. You should study these, as well as the brief examples already given, in order to develop the right skills. Of course, the *extraction* of *information* from sources is an essential skill, but is not usually a skill of a high order. The ability to read and understand the English language is not to be sneered at, but the ability to grasp the subtler nuances of meaning of a piece is much more commendable. Likewise, if you are to achieve a high assessment from your teacher and the Examining Group you will need to *compare* sources, both for what they contain and for what they omit, and to be able to express your comparison clearly. You will have to discuss the *bias*, the *reliability* and the *usefulness* of sources. Above all you will have to understand that no source is absolutely truthful and unbiased, but that all of them contain a *mixture* of the objective reality of what they were dealing with and the subjective influence of the individual who was the author.

Before looking at Chapter 2 to see how to set about choosing and researching a topic for coursework, it would be best to consider the requirements of the individual Examining Groups in a little more detail.

UNIT 4   COURSEWORK REQUIREMENTS OF THE EXAM GROUPS

4.1 London and East Anglian Group (LEAG)

The assessment objectives for coursework are mainly the same as those to be tested in the written examination. Nevertheless, the Group takes the view that objective 1 (concerned with recall and understanding of knowledge) is more appropriately tested in the written examination, whilst objective 4 (the ability to look at events from the perspective of people in the past, i.e. *empathy*) is usually more appropriately tested in coursework. As a result, the main concentration will be on assessment objectives 2, 3 and 4.

Coursework will account for 30% of the total marks. Three pieces of work will be required, one for each of the three objectives tested. The maximum for any one assignment will be 1500 words, with an overall maximum of 5000 words.

The assessment levels which the teacher should look for in marking the coursework are set out in detail for each of the various aspects of the assessment objectives. The following example lists the assessment levels for one aspect of assessment objective 2:

A study of continuity and change.
Target: The ability to describe and explain the factors involved in a changing historical situation and those factors which remain constant.
Level One: Gives a factual account of a situation or a series of events, the elements of change and continuity being identified only implicitly.
Level Two: Explains factors making for change and continuity.

Level Three: Makes some links between factors and compares with past or explains rate or nature of change.
Level Four: Emphasizes important factors, gives clear exposition of links and makes reasoned distinctions between major and minor factors.

Let us suppose we are dealing with changes and continuity as seen in town life in an industrial town in the north of England in the 1840s. You can see that a simple descriptive account (Level 1) of streets, buildings and people will not get you very far, even though you mention that some of the buildings are factories. Even if you make a list of the reasons for change, or explaining the lack of it (continuity), by saying that people are coming into the town looking for work, but blacksmiths are still doing the same work on horses as they always did, you will get only to Level 2. You have to *link* these changes into a coherent pattern by writing about the Industrial Revolution, the varying rates of technological change, and the impact all this makes on a town. This will get you to Level 3, but if you want to reach Level 4 your linking has to be clear and effective, and you have to make clear the relative importance of the points you are discussing (e.g. 'The industries where the rate of change was the greatest were those which mass-produced textiles or pottery for a rapidly growing market, and which offered the greatest opportunities for profit for enterprising manufacturers; whilst with others, on a smaller scale, with a market that was fixed or expanding only slowly, methods tended, as in thatching or silverware, to remain much more static.') The best answers would show how closely interlinked many of these factors were, until they cast clear light on the *nature* of change and continuity in a nineteenth-century town.

4.2 Midland Examining Group (MEG)

Coursework here will account for 30% of the marks in the whole examination. Each candidate is required to produce *one* or *two* pieces of coursework, but each may consist of a number of shorter pieces of work related to a common theme. This approach may be useful, as all four assessment objectives have to be demonstrated in the coursework, and this may be difficult to do in a single piece of work. Assignments are marked out of 100, and the four objectives are weighted somewhat differently: objective 1 scores 40, and the other three objectives 20 each.

There is said to be 'considerable discretion' in the presentation of coursework; whilst written pieces are accepted as the usual thing, coursework, with the Group's permission, may be submitted in the form of a videotape, an audiotape, a portfolio of photographs etc. The subject matter should be 'drawn from', or 'closely related to' the syllabus content as laid down in the Group's syllabus. The overall word limit is from 2000 to 4500 words.

Please note that assessment objective 1, which deals with the selection, arrangement and communication of historical knowledge, is rewarded with double the marks given to each of the other three objectives. The assessment levels for this objective are as follows:

Recall, selection, arrangement and communication of relevant knowledge.

Level 1: Mark range 1–3; shows the ability to select and use some relevant information to construct answers/narratives/descriptions which are accurate and reasonably thorough, but are likely to be relatively brief or limited in scope.
Level 2: Mark range 4–7; shows ability to select and use a wider range of relevant information in the construction of answers/narratives/descriptions which are accurate and reasonably thorough, but are nonetheless limited to the more obvious aspects of the matter under consideration.
Level 3: Mark range 8–10; shows ability to construct clear and detailed answers/narratives/descriptions based on thorough and accurate use of a wide range of factual material. Shows appreciation of wider context of information used.

Here, the differences between the various levels seem more self-explanatory. If you were writing about education in the Dames' Schools, for instance, you would get some credit for a simple short description based largely on the single source of what is in your textbook; but if you wanted to get to Level 2, you would have to use a wider range of sources, though still dealing with the most obvious aspects of the subject. Level 3 would require more sources still, but, more importantly, would expect you to deal with the less familiar aspects of the subject, or to put the Dames' Schools into the wider context of early nineteenth-century education. Whatever sources you were using, however, should be employed as *sources of information* in the course of your research; you should not merely copy chunks from one, followed by chunks from another. What many students fail to realize is that their teachers are probably familiar with a much wider range of sources than they are, and that many teachers will be able to *recognize* copied passages when they see them.

Note that the marks in the example above are given as out of 10. These would have to be scaled up and given out of 20 if there were only two pieces of work; in the less likely event that you were presenting one, the mark, of course, would be out of 40.

4.3 Northern Examining Association (NEA)

For this Group, four to six pieces of coursework are required. Between them, they should test all four of the coursework objectives. No assignment should be used to test more than *two* objectives at the same time. At least *one* assignment must be based on *each* of the four themes of the syllabus. These are:

1 Industrialization
2 Urbanization
3 Responses to industrialization, and
4 Social improvements

All assignments are allowed to draw on local history, or on local examples where appropriate. To gain high marks, these assignments are expected to reach a total of 3000 words, but not more than 6000 words. Coursework will count for 30% of the marks for the whole examination. It will be marked out of a total of 60, with an equal weighting of 15 marks being given to each of the assessment criteria.

Normally, written work will be the medium of the coursework assignments, but the Group is anxious that both candidates and teachers should have a degree of freedom in methods and styles of presentation. Hence the use of films, diagrams, models, tape-recordings, (audio and video) and dossiers of photographs will be accepted, so long as it is the work of the individual candidate. Where non-written work is undertaken, the end-product must be retained by the centre or by the individual candidate for any subsequent inspection and moderation. Assignments have to be ready for moderation by the end of April in the year of the examination.

4.4 Northern Ireland Schools Examinations Council: Modular (NISEC)

Coursework will be awarded 20% of the total marks for the examination. It will consist of three assignments, covering all the assessment objectives. The assignments will be based on Local Studies. They should be designed to permit students to demonstrate their ability to undertake a historical enquiry, to develop historical reasoning, and to express their knowledge and understanding through the medium of local history. The study can relate to the student's immediate local environment, *or* to an environment in Ulster but removed from the student's own environment, *or* it can deal with Ulster as a whole. Amongst the suggested topics for such local enquiries are:

1 The study of an aspect of agriculture, e.g. a 19th-century farm,
2 The study of an aspect of industry, e.g. Barbour Threads of Lisburn,
3 The study of an aspect of transport, e.g. Newry Canal, Giant's Causeway Railway, or
4 The study of an aspect of education, e.g. the schools of the area.

The study chosen may relate to the wider world, but should develop the Ulster connection, and study its impact within the Ulster context, e.g. Ulster linen manufacture could be seen in the context of the UK textile industry.

The first assignment is one of 750–1000 words, and tests assessment objective 1, 'to recall and select knowledge relevant to the context and deploy it in a clear and coherent form.' The assignment should communicate historical knowledge and understanding of the chosen topic, and present a sequential narrative which gives a clear and accurate description of the matter and the people it deals with.

In addition to this the assignment will also require students to comment, in general terms, on the range of evidence used for the study. This should include both *primary* and *secondary* sources, artefacts and 'orally-transmitted information'. It carries 8% of the total of 20% set aside for coursework, the knowledge and communication part scoring 5% of the marks, i.e. 25 marks and the scope of evidence part scoring 3%, i.e. 15 marks.

The second and the third assignments each carry 6% of the total of 20% coursework allocation. Each should be 500–700 words in length. The second concerns itself chiefly with assessment objectives 2 and 4. The former deals with cause and consequence/continuity and change/similarity and difference; the latter involves undertaking a specific study on the reliability of evidence which normally will take the form of a structured exercise. Objective 2 will score 4% of the marks, i.e. 20 marks, and objective 4 will score 2%, i.e. 10 marks.

The third assessment will be concerned with assessment objectives 3 and 4. The former deals with empathy and asks students 'to show an ability to look at events and issues from the perspective of people in the past'. The latter will include an analysis of 'various types of historical evidence, and reaching conclusions based on this comparison'. Objective 3 will score 4% of the marks, i.e. 20 marks, and objective 4 will score 2%, i.e. 10 marks.

All kinds of assignment can employ maps, diagrams, drawings, photographs etc., as well as written material, *provided that these other media of presentation help to answer the question*. Whatever the assignment, a similar system of levels of response will be employed. The assessment levels for objective 3, for example, are as follows:

Level 1: 0–5 marks. Candidates will be able to demonstrate knowledge of the perspective of people in the past, supported by general statement or disconnected specific examples.

Level 2: 6–11 marks. Candidates will be able to demonstrate knowledge and understanding of events and issues from the perspective of people in the past, supported by general statement or specific (*but no longer disconnected*) examples.

Level 3: 12–16 marks. Candidates will be able to demonstrate knowledge and understanding of events and issues from the perspective of people in the past which is supported by specific examples and *shows awareness of the complexity of perspectives*.

Level 4: 17–20 marks. Candidates will be able to demonstrate knowledge and understanding of events and issues from the perspective of people in the past which is *extensively* supported and which shows a *clear awareness* of the complexity of perspectives.

Though expressed in a form of words that is different from the formula expressed on page 5, the *incline of attainment* can clearly be seen here, and approximates very closely to the same idea as on the earlier page.

4.5 Southern Examining Group (SEG)

This Group requires two pieces of coursework, neither of them to exceed 1000 words in length. One must be concerned with assessment objective 3 (empathy), the other with assessment objective 4 (the use of a wide range of sources). Coursework carries 20% of the marks for the whole examination.

Assignments may be written in essay style or, in the case of sources, will be in the form of structured exercises. It is assumed that candidates will do a larger number of coursework assignments and that the best two will be submitted for examination assessment.

The same incline of attainment may be seen in the levels of response as in the case of the Northern Ireland example above. For instance, the assessment levels for objective 4 are as follows:

Level 1: Comprehension of source.
For example, extract plausible if only partly relevant information from source; extract relevant specific related information from more than one source. *(1–2 marks)*
Level 2: Simple interpretation and evaluation.
For example, classify one type of source, comment on nature and tone of information provided; comment on plausibility of source. *(3–4 marks)*
Level 3: Supported interpretation/evaluation of source.
For example, evaluate source by general sense of the period, in terms of the author's situation or purpose, or by process of cross-referencing; use of source not as information. *(5–7 marks)*
Level 4: Full appreciation of the nature of historical evidence.
For example, recognizing accounts may vary because of the nature of the sources on which they draw; identifying the relationship of the historian to the object of study; recognizing the nature of historical proof. *(8–10 marks)*

The extraction of information from sources will score low marks (Level 1) unless it is backed by the ability to classify the sources as primary or secondary, and to comment on the *kind* of source, the quality of its information and its likely reliability. Even this will reach only Level 2, and so obtain less than half the available marks. For Level 3 you will have to comment on the author's purpose in writing the source, be able to see the source in its historical context, compare it with other sources (*cross-referencing*), and see historical sources as *evidence* rather than as *information*. If you want to reach Level 4, you will have to go further than this: you will have to see your sources in the wider historical context, e.g. against the attitudes common in their time, and be able to assess their effectiveness as evidence, e.g. making allowances for the assumptions of their time. Examples of different levels of historical abilities will be found in Chapters 4 and 5.

4.6 Welsh Joint Education Committee: Modular (WJEC)

The social and economic aspects of this syllabus are not tested in coursework, but in the examination papers set, e.g. in parts of Paper 1, Paper 2 and Paper 3. The part to be studied in coursework (Module 4) is concerned with a Modern World Study, which is not in the area of Social and Economic History. Fuller details are to be found in the printed syllabus of WJEC.

UNIT 5 COURSEWORK MANAGEMENT

You will, of course, be asked to submit *coursework* not solely in Social and Economic History, but in most other GCSE subjects as well. This means that from the start you will be a bit like the juggler who has to keep six or seven plates in the air at the same time. One may be easy. Two are tricky. Three are very difficult. Four and more may seem to be well-nigh impossible. This is perhaps the most serious practical problem that you will have to face in your educational career.

5.1 Planning your work

The fact is that from the start of your examination course, fairly soon after the beginning of your fourth year, you will have to plan your work carefully, to prevent it from piling up. Recognizing that other of your examination courses need coursework, and that in some subjects it plays an even larger part than it does in Social and Economic History, you will have to take every step to prevent yourself being overwhelmed by it. Keeping things under control ought perhaps to be your first and overriding priority. How is it to be achieved?

The most important thing is to learn to deal with coursework as it occurs. When you are given a topic, perhaps, the final date for completion seems a long way off, and the need for setting about it straight away does not immediately strike you. If it is a fortnight or a month away there perhaps seems to be no immediate need for action. What you have not realized, or (if you have realized it) fully taken into account, is that similar assignments are going to be set in other subjects, equally, if not more, demanding. Postponement may seem an attractive proposition now, but when there are several assignments, all clamouring for your attention simultaneously, the prospects will seem much more threatening. You have to remember that even with the best will in the world you can only take on one job at a time.

TIMING

You ought to make special efforts to deal with the coursework promptly, and approach it steadily and systematically, instead of in unpredictable bursts. Above all, do not leave it until just before the closing date. You ought to take great care not to fall into the trap in which many students find themselves – namely that of regarding a *last* date as a *first* one. It is really much easier to plan to submit your work early than it is to leave it late: the embarrassment involved in making excuses is more wearing than the efforts of getting the work in on time, or before time. If, for instance, you have a fortnight in which to do separate tasks in three different subjects, you should not leave all of them until the start of the week in which they are due; that way either one or more of them will be skimped or neglected altogether. Try to turn to the work as *soon* as possible, not as *late* as possible; in that way you will undoubtedly do better work.

5.2 Enjoying your work

The question is also, oddly enough, one of enjoyment. No one can enjoy a task that is hurried, whether it is out of an examination, or in it. Part of the underlying purpose of the GCSE examination is to enhance the feelings of students that study is a good thing in itself, not solely as a way of getting examination qualifications, but as improving the qualities of their minds, and to lead them to take a pleasure in something which previously was an obligation and nothing more. That seems to many people to be a sure way not only of producing better work, but also of taking a positive pleasure in doing it.

CHAPTER ONE COURSEWORK MANAGEMENT

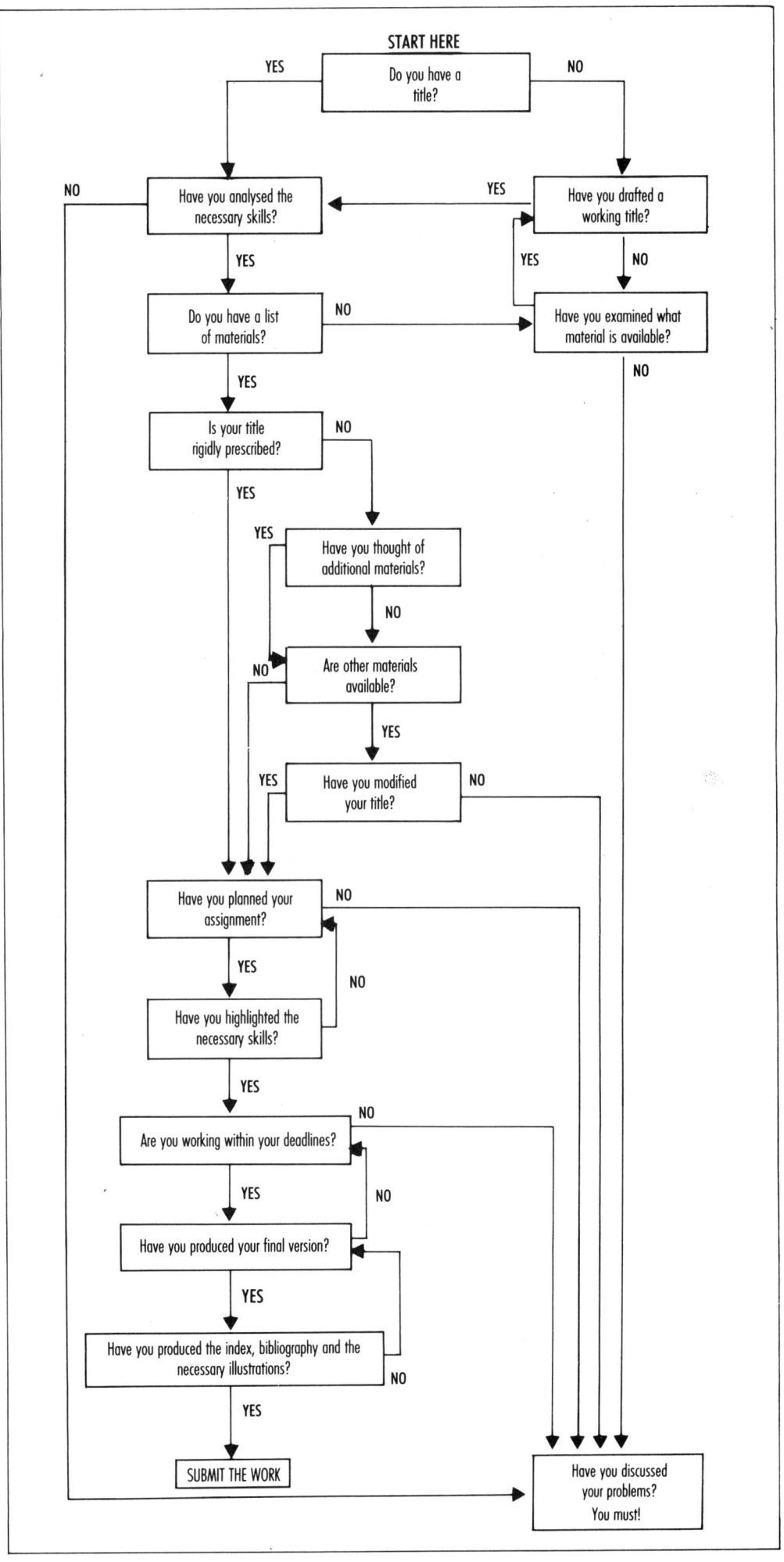

Fig 1.1

RESEARCHING A TOPIC

UNIT 1 — CHOOSING A TOPIC AND A TITLE

❝ What kind of assignment is it? ❞

In most cases you will find that your teacher will help you with your choice of assignment topic, and may well suggest a title. Indeed, the advance vetting of coursework by the groups may make *student selection* of coursework topics difficult and unlikely. Where there is room for you to have some say in the choice, you should be *guided by your teacher's advice*, since teachers are likely to have considerable experience of what is required, and to know what is possible within the limits of an average assignment.

The *nature of the topic chosen* should first be seen in relation to the *type of skills* which the assignment is intended to demonstrate. One that is intended to show your ability to handle a range of historical sources, to extract information from them, to compare them, to indicate gaps and inconsistencies in them, to detect bias, and so on, should be based on a number of pieces of evidence sufficiently substantial and numerous to be adequate for the task. You cannot, for example, make any comparison between documents unless there are at least two of them.

❝ Look at the flowchart on page 15 ❞

An assignment that is intended as an *empathy* exercise should seek to avoid all the obvious pitfalls inherent in this kind of work. Choose a topic that allows you to give several, and often conflicting, viewpoints. It might not be easy in an assignment on trade unionists to show people with various views, especially, for example, if they were members of the Dorset Agricultural Labourers Union in 1833–4. Unless you have access to local sources which showed divisions within the union, it might be better and easier to go for a more rewarding choice such as the Chartists. Even here it would be foolish to stereotype the two groups of 'moral force' and 'physical force' Chartists. You would need to show that within Chartism there was a wide variety of opinion.

An assignment intended to show your familiarity with *historical concepts* such as change and continuity, or similarity and difference, or one which demonstrates your *historical judgment* or your capacity to *evaluate*, should also be carefully chosen for this purpose. You will find examples of these in Chapters 4 and 5.

The demands of the assignment should be clear from the title, and there should be sufficient scope within the title for these demands to be met. Examples of three types of assignment – and there may be many others – will help clarify and develop these points.

1.1 Documentary assignments

If an exercise is based on documents chosen from the point of view of a possible *comparison*, the documents should clearly provide ample opportunity for a comparison to be made. Two such documents could be employed, for example, to illustrate the different attitudes towards female labour in factories during the parliamentary debates of 1844.

❝ Is it based on evidence extracts? ❞

I have, moreover, the authority of a millowner, that, if the present system of labour be persevered in, the 'county of Lancaster will speedily become a province of pygmies'. The toil of females has hitherto been considered the characteristic of life among savages; but we, in the height of our refinement, impose on the wives and daughters of England a burden from which, at least during pregnancy, they would be exempted even in the slave-holding states (of the USA), and among the Indians of America. But all these considerations are nothing compared with the moral mischiefs this system creates and sustains.

from Lord Shaftesbury's speech, Committee Stage, March 1844.

The noble lord said, the time is come when, in his opinion, it is necessary to lay the axe to the root of the tree. Before we do this let me entreat the Committee carefully to consider what is that tree which we are to fell. If it be, as I suppose, the tree of the commercial greatness of this country, I am satisfied that although some of its fruits may be bitter, yet upon the whole it has produced that greatness, that wealth, that prosperity, which makes these small islands most remarkable in the history of the civilised world, which upon the whole spread happiness amidst this great community, and make this nation one of the most civilised, if not the most civilised, and powerful on the face of the globe.

from Sir J. R. Graham's speech to the same Committee, March 1844.

These extracts could provide material for questions requiring further information or *recall*, such as 'Why did the millowner think that Lancaster could soon be a province of pygmies?' or 'What does Shaftesbury's speech say is wrong with female labour?' There could be a question about why Graham opposes a reduction in working hours for factory labourers. But the most important value of the two extracts lies in the possibility for comparison of the two viewpoints.

It is important to remember that a comparison of viewpoints must be *document-based*. It is not enough to make comparisons that are based solely on what you have been told about the documents, and to say for instance that the first is by the famous humanitarian Lord Shaftesbury, and the other is by Sir James Graham, whom you have looked up and discovered was a member of the government of that time. Such information would be useful, especially to point out that the government, through Graham, appeared opposed to Shaftesbury's proposed legislation. But these points are made only from the *attributions*, i.e. the labels attached to a particular passage to show where it came from, *who* said it and *when* it was said. Use of attributions must certainly be made, and valuable information can be deduced from comparing the dates of extracts and checking the backgrounds of speakers and seeking out the significance of places. Yet effective comparisons must be based, not on these attributions alone, but on the *contents* of the documents themselves.

Sometimes, the comparison depends on the different use of language. Here, Shaftesbury does use some vocabulary to heighten the effect; he talks of speedily, toil, refinement, savages and moral mischiefs – all of which are intended to win the support through emotive language which he may have failed to win over by logical argument elsewhere in his speech. Sir James Graham may not appear to you to be doing anything similar; but what is the cumulative effect upon the listener of the repetition of *greatness* and *civilised* (several times) and the notion of wealth and prosperity? The use of such words and phrases reveal the prejudices and bias of each speaker, i.e. his willingness to win an instinctive and unthinking approval from his supporters by loading the argument with judgments built into the vocabulary.

The main comparison here will, however, be one of *content*. Shaftesbury uses two arguments here; one, quoted from another source, about the stunting effect of factory work in Lancashire – surely an argument for banning factory employment altogether, rather than seeking a modest reduction in hours? And the other, a blatant appeal to the emotions about the employment of women, especially pregnant ones, and their exposure to moral danger. The moral argument is an especially powerful weapon of all humanitarians, and likely to succeed with the virtuous Victorians where other arguments would fail. Sir James does not attempt to compete with Lord Shaftesbury in the emotional 'minefield'. He carefully avoids reference to the sufferings of children and female factory workers, and in particular he makes no attempt to deny their suffering, even making a passing nod towards it in his reference to some of the fruits being 'bitter'. But his argument appeals to a Victorian characteristic almost as strong as the moral indignation so skilfully exploited by Shaftesbury – greed. In other words, if factory restrictions are imposed, the wealth and prosperity of the country – more important than any incidental human suffering – could be damaged.

The two documents, of course, give opposite sides of the picture, but they are not necessarily contradictory. Both views could be valid: factory work is inhuman; factory work is necessary. A good comparison will seek to bring out and to illustrate the main points each speaker is making. Background information will be needed; the factory legislation prior to 1844 will need to be looked at, and the Shaftesbury proposals of 1844 compared with the legislation of that year. But this is not like a context question in English Literature, and does not require or involve the use of extensive background information. To a large extent your answer will be built up from the material in the two documents themselves. In using this material you should not be afraid to employ selected quotations, if these illustrate your points well. This does not mean that you should copy out the passages in their entirety to avoid missing some shadow of meaning; the exercise is one of *selection* in picking out the most useful words and phrases.

This exercise is a comparison between two contemporary and *similar pieces of historical evidence*; documents of much the same length and serving a comparable purpose. They are not in themselves substantial enough to form a complete assignment; more, or longer, extracts would be needed, with more questions, to fulfil this requirement. You can, of course, use more than just documentary extracts in your assignment. It would be possible, for instance, to compare two different Punch cartoons dealing with a similar subject. It is also possible to compare together *different sorts of evidence*. A documentary passage could be compared with a cartoon – how far is the message of the cartoon in sympathy with the views of either of the speakers? A variety of other sorts of historical evidence (contemporary engravings or illustrations, maps, graphs, statistics, etc.) can also be employed.

It is unlikely that you will yourself be wholly responsible for choosing the evidence for this kind of exercise. But where you do have some influence, you should take care to choose the documents that are the most appropriate for the exercise.

1.2 Empathetic assignments

> **Does it involve empathy?**

These provide you with an opportunity to demonstrate your ability to look at events and issues from the perspective of people in the past. This type of exercise is intended to combine two elements: your historical knowledge, and the acuteness of your historical perception. Such exercises have now been largely removed from the examination, because coursework offers greater opportunities for a convincing demonstration of empathy, based on a wide variety of authoritative evidence. Nevertheless, care should be taken with the *choice* of empathetic subjects; a bad choice of title could limit your chances of reaching the highest assessment level.

To illustrate this point, we shall consider some possible empathetic titles:

1 As a landowner, explain your reasons for supporting the enclosure of your village which is proposed to take place in 1795. It will be necessary for you to convince a parliamentary committee to let enclosure go ahead, despite the opposition of many of the villagers.
2 How would Vansittart, the Chancellor of the Exchequer in 1815, have sought to convince the Cabinet that it was right to abolish the income tax?
3 The mayor of Birmingham is to make Lord Shaftesbury a freeman of the borough in 1880 on account of his efforts to improve factory conditions. What comparisons would the mayor make of factory conditions in the 1830s and 1870s, and what improvements would he attribute to Lord Shaftesbury?
4 Write an article for an important daily newspaper on the death of Sir Edwin Chadwick in 1890, explaining his importance in the development of the Poor Law and Public Health.
5 Explain the arguments in favour of Free Trade in the 1840s, and the arguments against it at that time. In view of Britain's economic development during the second half of the nineteenth century, do you think that Britain was right to adopt Free Trade during the 1850s and 1860s?
6 What sort of arguments would have been put forward at a public meeting in 1840 to decide whether or not to oppose local plans to build a railway?

Which of these titles *fails* to fulfil the essential requirements of an empathetic assignment, and for what reasons? Look again at number 5, and consider it from this point of view. There are two reasons for rejecting this title. In the first place it is *analytical* and *descriptive* instead of being empathetic. It is perfectly possible to have memorised the arguments for and against Free Trade, without attempting to empathise with them. Furthermore, the second part of the question, demanding hindsight from the point of view of the contemporary scene, fails in the key requirement of 'looking at events and issues from the perspective of people in the past'. To choose this title might therefore present you with considerable difficulties.

Titles 1 and 3 both require you to put yourself in the place of someone in the past – the landowner, or the mayor of Birmingham – and to see a particular situation in the way that person would have seen it at the time, speaking as he would have spoken, and arguing in the way he would have argued. The weakness here does not lie in the nature of the subject-matter, though some people would argue that it is very one-sided to see enclosure from the landowner's point of view. (The same people would, however, probably approve of seeing things through the eyes of an underprivileged cottager, which shows how easily history can forfeit the impartiality it is so proud of possessing!) The real criticism of these titles is that they require you to impersonate an *imaginary historical person*, and speculate about the way such a character would have behaved. Such an exercise is said to be *role-play*, and is generally now believed to be a rather artificial and even fanciful one. Furthermore, it is a *one-dimensional* exercise, since it provides only an individual opinion, and conveys none of the diversity of contemporary opinion existing on any historical subject.

Title 2, requiring you to put yourself into Vansittart's shoes, at least involves a *real historical person* instead of an imaginary one. But it shares some of the weaknesses of the role-play exercises. In particular it is again *one-dimensional*, since it will offer the opinions only of a single individual, and can provide little indication of the differing political opinions about the abolition of the income tax. Indeed, the pitfalls of such an answer may be even greater; no-one can say with certainty that you are wrong in the way you interpret the thinking of an *imaginary* person, but the problem about impersonating a *real* person, and an eminent one, is that you may easily be accused of *misrepresenting* him. You would need to be very familiar indeed with biographies of Vansittart to be sure that you were not, in your attempt to unload on him all the arguments against the income tax, crediting him with arguments he would never have uttered. There is also the further pitfall in this case (which you could easily overlook) that the sort of arguments which might have been used in the cabinet may bear only a limited resemblance to those designed for wider public consumption.

Title 4 is also about a *real historical character*, but at least it concerns him at *second-hand* and not at first-hand, since it is about how an imaginary newspaper editor would have written about Chadwick. Part of the weakness here is that it is perfectly possible to give a factual account of the changes he brought about without any *empathetic* interpretation of his role. Another potential weakness is that the judgment on his achievements in 1890 could be seen as much the same as a judgment made in the 1990s. There is therefore no *guarantee* that the answer you give to this question will be regarded as empathetic.

Answers to a title such as 4 above therefore have two possible faults: first, they represent the views of a single, imaginary newspaper editor, and are *one-dimensional*; second, they are more analytical than empathetic. Nevertheless, it is worth observing that good empathy *could* be written in answer to this question, and of the five titles examined so far, this is probably the most effective. Part of such an article could be written on the lines suggested below:

Opinions vary on the merits of the changes Chadwick was responsible for. There are those who would argue that his part in condemning outdoor relief for the able-bodied led thousands into the misery of the workhouse. But that was not necessarily his intention. If, as some argue, he forced farmers to pay their labourers a living wage in order to keep them out of the workhouse, then he deserves universal praise, not condemnation. On the other hand, it may be conceded that he did much to arouse concern for public health, but some feel that he was indifferent to the liberty and property of individuals, and rode roughshod over them to achieve his aims, regardless of who or what was in the way.

Development of this style of treatment shows *various viewpoints*, and if sustained would be classed as *differentiated empathy*.

Of all the six titles, however, *number 6* is clearly the most appropriate for the purpose. Weak answers, of course, could still be written on this topic. A student might produce a list of arguments for and against railways which had been memorised or copied from note-lists, and containing nothing which could be identified as empathy. Worse still, these lists could be accompanied by an analysis which blames the railway opponents of 1840 for their shortsightedness in view of all the blessings railways were to confer during the rest of the century – an example of the hindsight approach which places empathy exercises firmly in Level 1. Even if students do tackle this from the viewpoint of 1840, they should be careful not to stereotype the two sides, i.e. they should not assume united and unanimous opposition from landowners, and united and unanimous support from local traders. The best answers will show a variety of opinion across the various local groups. Some landowners, even those who will lose land to the railway, may see some advantages in its coming other than merely their compensation. Other local groups will not necessarily support or oppose out of naked self-interest, but may see community benefits or disadvantages in having a railway. This approach would need to be developed in the depth and length necessary to meet the specific requirements of the relevant Exam Group.

Although it is desirable that coursework assignments directed towards empathy should be very carefully selected, empathy need not necessarily be confined to questions that are specifically designed to test it. *Any* extended piece of historical writing, if it shows a mastery of its subject, will probably have significant empathetic overtones. A good piece of *biographical work*, for example, on James Watt, will show a sensitive appreciation of the problems he faced both in improving Newcomen's engine, and in trying to turn his achievements into a business success. It will endeavour to look at Watt's problems in much the same way as Watt looked at them himself. Again, good work on tariff reform in the early twentieth century will show some ability in appreciating the point of view of *both sides*, and will not – unlike newspaper accounts – identify exclusively with one partisan viewpoint or the other. In other words, empathy may show itself in any historical writing concerned with personalities, events and situations.

1.3 Evaluation or assessment assignments

In this case, too, the choice of subject can be all-important. Again it may be useful to consider some possible titles:

1. British membership of the Common Market: how valuable has this been in the 1980s?
2. How effective has British aid been in stimulating the economies of Third World countries during the 1980s?
3. 'The nationalisation policies of the government in the late 1940s were morally justified and opposition to them was shortsighted and selfishly motivated.' Do you agree? Explain your answer carefully.

4 Pop culture.
5 How effectively did the government handle the economy during the Second World War?
6 'The years 1875–1914 were years of continuing and unbroken decline for British agriculture'. Do you agree?

Most of these titles attempt to examine a *particular historical problem*, in a way that is appropriate for an assignment of the length required. In choosing a topic, it is extremely important *not* to select a title that is purely narrative or descriptive, such as the following:

7 The history of the suffragettes.
8 What were the main developments in the iron industry during the years 1750 to 1850?

❝ Does it involve evaluation or assessment? ❞

Details of both these subjects can be found in secondary texts, so that by borrowing passages from carefully selected accounts you could produce respectable answers without much effort. This 'scissors and paste' method is frowned upon by GCSE assessors; it defeats the underlying motive of the assessment, which is to stimulate some (admittedly limited) research activity by candidates. Topics ought to cover something *more manageable* and *more precise*. This enables you to explore more thoroughly a particular corner of history, and, rather than repeating what *others have already found*, make your *own* contribution to the examination of the problem. Your title may even take the form of a question, in order to provide a sharper focus to the issue under consideration.

Nevertheless, considerable difficulties remain for an evaluation assignment, and it is helpful to be aware of them in advance. Examine the six titles suggested at the head of this section and see if you can work out what these difficulties are.

Title 1 refers to recent events, is topical and will probably yield plenty of statistics and diagrams which can be used or adapted for your work. The trouble arises from the use of the word 'valuable' in the second part of the title. Valuable for whom, or for what? It is likely to mean how valuable to Britain, but it could also mean how valuable to the Common Market itself.

However, the answer to this question is largely a matter of individual opinion, and in a problem of this kind you will probably find that even the economic experts cannot agree. This is not, in effect, a historical question but an economic one. And in terms of 'value' it is certainly possible to check British exports to, and imports from, the Common Market, but in that case all that 'valuable' means is a statistical measure of trade. Yet the value to Britain of EEC membership surely involves a good deal more than this; and it is the attempt to assess this extra value that takes the answer out of history into political controversy.

A similar problem confronts us in Title 2. The purpose and extent of aid to the Third World is very much a matter of political controversy, and since useful evidence here will be very hard to find, the answer is likely merely to be the candidate's opportunity to display his political convictions and prejudices. Such topics as these should be avoided. There is no effective statistical means of quantifying the precise stimulating effect of Britain's aid to Third World countries, and speculative answers are hardly likely to show much historical skill.

'Moral justification', in Title 3, makes the question impossible to answer. What appeared to be moral justification to one person would be seen quite differently by another. In the same way, an observer who *approved* of the Labour government's nationalisation policies would be able to show that Britain's desperate economic plight after the war needed a new approach. On the other hand, an opponent of nationalisation could point out the dangers of risking all by change, experimentation and party dogma. Both supporters and opponents of nationalisation have a moral case. How, then, can it be determined historically? And who is to judge upon the validity of a candidate's answer? Such questions are best not set, and best left alone if set.

Title 4 opens up new problems. There is no doubt that 'pop culture' is an important part of social history and features in several syllabuses, but as it stands, the topic is far too wide to be covered in a GCSE coursework assignment. Fashionable though it is, the title is loose and indeterminate. There is no limitation of period or country, although as this is a British Economic and Social History syllabus the assumption is that the 'pop' will be British; yet so much 'pop' is international, and not exclusively British. Nor is the question restricted to a manageable and more clearly defined area of the 'pop' world. Furthermore, the assignment is not a historical investigation; there is no exploration of concept or causality. Presumably the candidate will select and describe anything that seems appropriate, and so there will be no evaluation or analysis and historical context will be lacking. If it becomes merely a description of recent or contemporary art forms it will cease to have any real historical value, and it will thus serve no useful purpose as a coursework assignment, no matter how enthusiastically the candidate chooses to write about a favourite rock group.

The subject matter of Title 5, on the other hand, is *limited* and *distinctive enough* to be chosen as the topic of an assignment. It is not too difficult to pin-point the economic problems facing the government: the maintenance of food supplies and their fair distribution; the allocation of scarce resources and the balancing of military and civilian needs; the problems of manpower bearing in mind the needs of the armed forces and of agriculture and industry; the danger of inflation; the funding of our international payments, particularly to the USA; and the maintenance of an effective wartime transport system.

You will no doubt think of a number of others, and may well wonder whether this assignment, too, should not have been narrowed down. But the overall picture of Britain's economy in war is a more valuable exercise than tackling two or three specific war problems in isolation. One skill that could be demonstrated here is that of presenting a balanced selection of themes, material and argument. There is a lot of evidence about government policy in government circulars and instructions of the period. Many secondary texts contain valuable statistics which indicate the effectiveness, or otherwise, of these policies. And if you can find elderly adults with good wartime memories, you may be able to tape-record valuable *first-hand* commentaries on rationing, direction of labour, shortages of consumer goods, restrictions on travelling and many other relevant matters. Do remember not to get carried away. This exercise is on *economic policy*, and lengthy reminiscences about the Blitz and the Home Guard may be fascinating, but are probably of only marginal relevance. You should remember too that the recollections of individuals can become dimmed and inaccurate with the passage of years. Nevertheless, you will find County Record Offices with useful wartime material, national as well as local (written documents, letters, photographs, official information and so on) and you may find useful information on how the nation's wartime economic problems affected local factories, mines or agriculture. It is quite possible that you will make a worthwhile and interesting contribution, although a modest one, to historical research, and that others later following your lead, will be able to do the same thing in their own localities.

The same is true of Title 6. Again, if you live in an agricultural area, local information could prove very helpful, and there are plenty of secondary accounts and published sources containing valuable statistics on prices of agricultural commodities and acreages under cultivation. This is a somewhat controversial topic: its phrasing should alert you to be cautious. Historical statements suggesting an unrelieved and unbroken trend usually require modification as this one does. Beware also of historical statements using *never* and *always*: they, too, will almost certainly require to be challenged. Another danger is to assume that local conditions will be reflected nationally. It would be foolish to assume because of the growth of market gardening in Essex that there was no agricultural depression. Your local sources suggest a way in which the national picture might be modified, but it does not mean that farmers nationwide were growing rich on the sale of greenhouse lettuce. Here, you would be looking at a problem that taxes economic historians at the highest level. Your modest ideas may not influence the historical debate, but you will have studied something worthwhile, gained a good deal from it, and made your own small contribution to historical knowledge.

Provided enough thought and care is devoted to choosing a good subject, both *national* and *local* themes can be studied in a history assignment without resorting to mechanical methods of 'scissors and paste'.

Questions can only be usefully dealt with, of course, when the *evidence is available* to enable them to be answered. You may find that you have asked a question which simply cannot be answered. In cases such as this – and there may be quite a number – you have no choice but to *modify the question* until it *can* be answered. This process, especially if repeated, can move you some way from your original point of departure. You may even have to abandon your enquiry altogether, and seek another starting point.

PROCEDURES

A useful *procedure*, therefore, for such an evaluation/assessment assignment, i.e. one in which you have a choice of subject, would be as follows:

1. *Select* a general area of enquiry, and construct a working question.
2. Collect your *research material*, using footnote references in one book to lead you to another. List and make a note of archive references to the local County Record Office (CRO) where these are available and relevant.
3. *Modify* your working questions in the light of the contents of your research findings. When you have arrived at a question which you believe can be effectively answered, settle on your final title.
4. Set out the steps by which the question can be answered as *separate sections* of your work, and rough out the intended contents of each of these sections.
5. Write a *draft* of each of these sections and produce the first draft of your assignment. Satisfy yourself that you have adequately answered your question.
6. Write out your assignment in its *final form*, providing it with a title page, a table of contents, a bibliography (list of titles and authors of books consulted), and an index, and

inserting any illustrations, photographs etc. Remember that this is *not* a photograph album, and that your text should not be overloaded with illustrations. (An unlikely exception in economic and social history would occur where the subject-matter of your assignment dealt specifically with the photograph coverage of a specific occurrence.)
7 Always work well within your *deadlines* and set yourself intermediate deadlines for the stages mentioned above. This avoids rushing the final version of the work.

The selection and development of a subject should provide you with an enjoyable, as well as a fruitful, enterprise. At all stages you should *consult with your teacher* and take heed of any advice you are given, as he or she may sometimes identify flaws or make suggestions that you would not necessarily have thought of for yourself. Remember too that it is your teacher who is going to assess the mark and award a mark for it.

The stages outlined here relate to a *project* which is a major piece of coursework, though they can be applied to other, shorter pieces of work. It is not necessary for those who have to produce assignments of 800–1000 words (as for SEG) to produce an index, but it might be desirable where the coursework consists of one major piece of writing. In the vast majority of cases your teacher will be setting the assignments and providing the sources, although there will still be some scope for individual students to seek out further material.

UNIT 2 SOURCES OF INFORMATION

In many cases students will find themselves provided with copies of historical source material by their teachers, or at least with some indication where this material can be found. Nevertheless, it will be useful if you know a little about these sources on your own account. What follows is general guidance on the subject of the *location and use of historical source material*.

2.1 Libraries

Most students will be able to use their *school or college library*, and have access to the material stored there. It is, however, important to join other libraries as well – which in most cases will mean the *local public library*. Although there may be a small joining fee, the services of these libraries are otherwise free.

When you are familiar with the layout of libraries you will see that they provide you with access to a good deal of valuable source material. They are chiefly organised into three sections:

▶ **borrowing facilities**, which enable you to remove books from the premises to study at your leisure (though with a stated limit on the period of borrowing);
▶ **reference facilities**, which enable you to consult books without removing them (although many reference departments have excellent reprographic machines which allow you to take photocopies of important pages to use for study purposes);
▶ **inter-library loan services**, which enable you to secure books not available in your library by borrowing them from other libraries. This is a very important facility if your local library is a branch library with only limited resources. It will be able to obtain books quickly from the central library of your town or county, and if necessary within a matter of weeks from libraries in other parts of the country.

You will find that libraries provide you with the following sources:

Books
Articles in handbooks, encyclopaedias etc.
Yearbooks
Periodicals and newspapers

BOOKS

At first sight, the vast numbers of books in a public library may seem daunting, and first of all you must learn your way about. If you are unfamiliar with the layout of a library, especially if it is a large one, it will help to spend a little time wandering round the shelves and getting to know the general location of the material. You will also learn that you are expected to be reasonably quiet, and to be considerate of the needs and interests of other library users.

The Dewey Classification

For coursework purposes, you will find it is the *non-fiction* books in which you are interested. For convenience these are arranged in nearly all libraries into the *Dewey Classification*. Each book is given a classification number, which is displayed in most cases on its spine, and also prominently on the appropriate shelves. The Dewey Classification divides human knowledge into ten categories.

    000 General Works
    100 Philosophy
    200 Religion
    300 Social Sciences
    400 Languages
    500 Science
    600 Technology
    700 The Arts and Recreation
    800 Literature
    900 Geography, Biography and History

Each of these classes is sub-divided to specify subjects in greater detail. English history, for example, is classified as 942 and may be further sub-divided in accordance with period and subject matter, e.g. 942.789; the higher the last three figures, the later the period. Biographies often have the first three letters of the subject's name added, for example TEL for Telford. This makes it easier to find books in a closely-packed biographical section.

To discover whether a library has the book you require, you should learn to use the *card index*, or, in modern libraries, the *microfiche index*. Both of these record all the books the libraries hold in alphabetical order, both by author and title. Using the index is the best way to find out whether a library has a copy of a given book, since you can hunt along the shelves a long time without finding it – or it may have been taken out by a previous borrower. There are other ways of tracing the existence of books, for example through the use of a *cumulative book index*, but these are more difficult, and will probably require you to ask the librarian on duty for help. Asking the librarian is often a good idea, especially if you do not have specific books in mind, but want to know what the library has to offer in relation to your assignment theme. Librarians are only too keen to help, but you should try not to be too vague:

Student: 'Have you any books on British Economic History?'
Librarian: 'What period?'
Student: 'I'm not sure: I think something on the Industrial Revolution would do.'

This kind of request is unlikely to fire the imagination of the librarian, and may well induce irritation! The more specific you can be, the more likely it is that the librarian will find what you need.

Using books

Learning to find your way round a book is perhaps rather simpler. Most books have a *table of contents* in the front, and an *index* in the back to guide you to the places in the text where specific topics are covered. The index can also save you reading through a great deal of irrelevant material in search of a particular piece of information.

Many books also have, either at the front or end, a *bibliography* of the books used, or recommended, by the author. Some books contain further bibliographical references tucked away in footnotes scattered throughout the text. Bibliographies and footnotes can often alert you to further sources of information which you might otherwise have missed.

You should always remember, when making use of a book, to *record* the appropriate particulars in order to be able to refer back to them later. In the notes you have taken, you should attach details of the *title*, the *author*, and the *publisher* of the book, the *Dewey Classification* (where there is one), and the *pages* and *chapters* from which the notes came. There is nothing more annoying than taking notes from a book and not being able to refer back to it later because you have forgotten what book the notes were taken from. The same thing, incidentally, is true of archive and other sources: you should *always* note the index number in case you need it again at a later time.

Borrowing books

If, after a thorough search, you finally discover that the library does not have a copy of the particular book you need, then you could ask the inter-library loans service to obtain the book from the nearest library where it is held. Remember that although the inter-library services are very good, there is always a time-lag. Getting a book from within the county area may take several days, but getting one from further afield may well take from two to four weeks.

OTHER LIBRARY RESOURCES

Reference departments are organised in a similar way to lending departments. However, you cannot borrow the books they hold, but must consult them on the spot. Reference departments will hold, in addition to books of the ordinary type, encyclopaedias, dictionaries of biography (national and international), yearbooks, handbooks and the like. A number of them also keep periodicals on file, and possibly even daily newspapers.

Encyclopaedias

These are probably the most important reference sources, since the best of them combine the functions of an atlas, a gazetteer, a dictionary, a who's who and a compendium of knowledge. Although they are not designed for the specialist, you will find they provide very useful information. Probably the best of the encyclopaedias is the *Encyclopaedia Britannica*, which went through fourteen editions before the present editorial policy of continuous revision was introduced. You should refer to the front of the volume you are using to find out how old it is, so you can be sure that the information is fairly up-to-date. Other well-known encyclopaedias include *Chambers' Encyclopaedia*.

Dictionaries of dates

These are kept by a number of libraries, and may be useful in providing accurate information of this type. Reference books such as the Longman *Handbook of Modern British History* provide a great deal of material besides dates. There are student equivalents of publications like these, for instance the *Longman GCSE Reference Guides* in History.

Other reference books

It is impossible to list all the other reference books which you may find useful, but you ought to be aware of the existence of:

▶ *Keesing's Contemporary Archives*, which gives a brief digest of British and world news at frequent intervals, all of which are collected and bound together by libraries to give a contemporary summary of developments. There are other, simpler, versions of this production which are targeted on students of school age.
▶ *Statesman's Yearbook*, published annually, which provides detailed information and statistics, mostly arranged geographically.
▶ *Whitaker's Almanac*, also published annually, provides similar information.

Newspapers

These are kept in some library reference departments, although often back copies of only one or two national papers such as the *Times* or *Guardian* are kept. You may find, however, that back copies of local newspapers are on record, and these may well turn out to be useful in connection with a local assignment. Unfortunately, not all newspapers are equally reliable, and some, especially the local ones, do not always report events accurately. Hence, in using newspapers as sources, you should always be cautious in accepting their accounts. Many older newspapers are by this time in a fragile condition and should be handled very delicately for fear that they tear or crumble. For this reason, many libraries have put their newspapers on microfiche, and these are now read by means of a viewer (some with an inbuilt photocopying facility). If you wish to refer to a large number of newspapers, and you are fortunate enough to live in the London area, or are able to visit London, you could make a journey to the newspaper library at Colindale in North London, which has very extensive newspaper records.

Never be afraid to ask for the guidance of the *reference librarian* if you need it; this can save a great deal of wasted time in a vain search for a book or periodical. Librarians are always willing to help with genuine enquiries, so long as you take care to make your enquiry as clear as possible.

2.2 Archive sources

Archive sources

Nearly all county towns have a County Record Office, or CRO, a local repository of archive material. A number of these have already established close relations with schools and colleges, and have packaged materials which may be useful in the preparation of coursework assignments. Students living in London are also fortunate to have near at hand a number of national archive sources such as the *Public Record Office*, or PRO, but it is less likely that GCSE students would wish to use this.

It is best to be introduced to your local CRO properly, either by arranging a visit with your teacher, or asking your teacher for a letter of introduction. Archivists do not appreciate students wandering aimlessly through the record office without any clear idea of what they are doing. Many CROs issue membership cards to their users, and require visitors to sign the visitor's book at every visit, partly as a security precaution. All of them operate on strict rules: no coats or bags in the search room; documents to be signed for when collected from the searchroom supervisor; pencils only to be used in the searchroom; damage to, or markings on, documents to be avoided, and so on. You should also make sure you know the time when the CRO will be open, particularly if you have to travel some distance in order to visit it.

You will find that all the documents or group of documents in a CRO are carefully numbered and their particulars recorded in an extensive card index. This classifies them by subject matter and in other ways. There is little point in browsing through the index unless you have some idea of what you want. You should at least make clear your intentions to some extent before embarking on your trip. Your teacher or the archivist on duty will be able to give you a general idea of the strengths of the Office. This is the point from which you ought to begin, in order to find out what other material may be helpful.

When you have eventually located and used an archive source, you should carefully note its index number before returning it to the archivist. Put this in your notes along with the material you have noted from the source, so that you can easily refer to it again in the future if you need to.

You will find there are two main types of archive source which may be of value to you in your work: material with national connections, and local material.

MATERIAL WITH NATIONAL CONNECTIONS

Important national movements may have had an impact on your local area, and your CRO may have a good set of records showing this. You may, for example, find that the CRO is useful in offering material on the General Strike of 1926, or material on the campaign for Nuclear Disarmament in the 1950s, or the timing and extent of the decline of the cottage weaving industry in your area.

The wartime economy theme referred to above on page 20, of course, is an example of a national matter which was bound to have local implications. At the same time, it does not follow that any of these themes will be fully documented, even though the whole country was affected by shortages and economic restrictions, since there is often a 'hit-or-miss' quality about local records. Conversely, you may well be surprised to find that there are excellent records, even on a topic where you would not really have expected it! These documents may then be studied in conjunction with contemporary press records. A useful project title here would be: 'How did such and such a wartime economic policy affect Cityville or Loamshire during the early (middle/later?) stages of the war?'

LOCAL MATERIAL

Material that is purely of local importance may also be represented in the CRO. Sources to do with local experiences during the Depression, or the impact of war-time rationing, or the construction of a motorway may be available, and there may be good collections of material in the form of personal letters or diaries. There may be information relating to the history of a particular school or college, its rebuilding or closure.

You may find valuable sources of *social* history well represented. Slum clearance and rehousing is one such subject, where records may show how a population has been moved from one area of the town to another, to live in quite different situations and in different types of property. The records may highlight the differences that this move produces in the people's way of life as well as on the local maps. Other social themes may include changes in the employment pattern over the last fifty years, standards of living and living conditions before the war, the end of trams and trolley buses, local fairs and carnivals, and so on.

It is worth saying that what you will *not* find is material of fairly recent date. The records of when and how your school became a comprehensive school, for instance, will still be regarded as sufficiently sensitive not to have reached the public shelves; in the same way, matters relating to people who are still living will not be within your reach.

Suitable areas of study should be discussed with your teacher, who may well be able to link this primary archive material to secondary sources in the form of specialist books on housing, leisure habits and so on. If you have spent some time examining original source material, you should explain to your teacher exactly what information you have to hand, so that he or she can get some idea of whether your suggestion will work. It may well be that from the particular angle you have been following, *you know more than your teacher does on the subject.*

Archive material should be used to help you *reach conclusions* in your coursework assignments, but it should not merely be reproduced or summarised. The mere act of locating archive material and copying it is not especially creditworthy. Giving a summary of the contents of the documents and reproducing the archive material in appendices does not add significantly to the sum of historical knowledge. It is your job to *interpret* the material and relate it to the theme that you are investigating. After all, other people can easily locate the archive documents themselves: if all you do is to reproduce what the documents *say*, you have not made any important use of them.

You should bear in mind that the writers of general secondary texts may well be unfamiliar with the primary documentary material that you may find in archive sources such as CROs. To be able to bear out, or cast doubt on, an accepted interpretation is a valuable and original contribution to historical knowledge. This alone makes it worthwhile.

2.3 Museums

Like Record Offices, museums are also useful to the student of history; these may be *national museums*, to which your school may organise a trip.

SPECIALIST MUSEUMS

Using museums

Museums dealing in *specialist subjects*, in which you have an interest, are often best visited by yourself during holiday time. The museums at Halifax, where you could study the technological changes of the industrial and agrarian revolutions, are an example. There is also the *National Railway Museum* in York, which is useful in studying the development of rail transport; the *National Motor Museum* in Beaulieu could be used for a similar study of road transport during the motor age.

Of course, there are museums of a more *local character*, but which still deal with a specialist topic, like the *brewery museums* in Burton-on-Trent. These museums usually have useful collections of artefacts, backed by impressive photographic coverage of the subject, and a visit will almost certainly enable you to build up a useful collection of notes, as well as copies of the materials distributed by the museum. Your teacher will probably help you in working out a suitable subject for a coursework assignment in connection with any of the major collections of these museums.

NON-SPECIALIST MUSEUMS

Non-specialist municipal and county museums usually have good collections, quite often strong in social and economic history from the eighteenth century onwards. Local museums will also be especially valuable in providing material for a *local history assignment*, e.g. nineteenth century urban growth in the particular locality.

Visiting museums

The tendency in museums is to move away from carefully shielded displays in glass cases and towards what is sometimes called the 'hands-on experience'. That is to say, museum visitors are being increasingly invited to *handle* the exhibits and to get to know them by *feel*, instead of by studying them in the highly artificial context of a display cabinet. Thus, a nineteenth-century labourer's cottage collection might well include pots and pans, a fire range, appropriate furniture, a tin bath, a wash-board and small artefacts for you to examine in detail. Museums such as the Castle Museum in York and the Beamish Museum near Durham have period streets as well as period rooms from which an observant visitor can learn much about the way of life of previous generations.

Cassette or filmstrip programmes sometimes accompany collections on a particular topic. They may be studied at the museum, or taken away on loan for more detailed study at your leisure. These can provide a good deal of material for a coursework assignment.

This *raw material* for history assignments, of course, needs further supporting information, perhaps from primary or secondary sources in the archive offices and libraries. Remember that the assignment you eventually produce will be a piece of *written* work, and that written resources, as well as artefacts, will be needed to complete it.

2.4 Historical fieldwork

❝ Getting your feet wet ❞

It is sometimes said that it is a mistake to emphasise the use of *books* in the study of history at the expense of *boots*. Visits to local CROs may soon tempt you to turn from the situation as it exists in the records to that which exists on the ground. A comparison of two local maps in the record office, dating from 1910 and 1970 may make you think it would be a good idea to trace out the changes by *visiting* the areas illustrated. The closure of a local railway and its marking on the map as 'disused railway' may persuade you to walk along its former railbed and to take notes on it. Reading about slum clearance and rehousing in large towns may encourage you to visit both the cleared areas and the new areas of housing development. All this would be invaluable in supporting a local history assignment on railways or living conditions.

It is nearly always better to work *from* the records and *to* the visit rather than the other way round. You may find that a very interesting visit has little archival support for further study. It is much more sensible to check on the materials available first, and then to make a visit in order to extend your knowledge.

FIELDWORK TRIPS

Fieldwork may also be undertaken in more ambitious visits which your school may organise, perhaps to a useful historical site in the vicinity:

▶ If you want to know something more about trading ships and get the feel of what it must have been like to serve on one, visit one of the various ship museums, such as the *Cutty Sark* at Greenwich.
▶ If you want to know more about the life of civilians during the Second World War, visit the former prisoner-of-war camp at Malton in Yorkshire, now a museum specialising in this topic.

These are but two examples among many. Your *interests* and your *locality* will determine your museum choice, and your teacher will be able to recommend the most suitable.

SPECIALISED FIELDWORK

Fieldwork of a special kind could be used to support some of the projects mentioned above, namely *oral history*. Using a portable tape-recorder, you could interview elderly relatives and their friends and get them to answer questions, or to recount their experiences during the Depression or to describe civilian life during the Second World War. A certain amount of forethought and planning is necessary here. More than one testimony is clearly preferable to a single one; indeed, the more the better.

You should *discuss the proposal with your teacher*, and *plan a questionnaire* for the main points to be covered. Try to keep your witnesses to the point while they are answering, but at the same time avoid interrupting them too frequently, and try to talk as little as possible yourself. Oral history has the great advantage of immediacy, but it also has significant weaknesses. People may have forgotten what really happened, or, worse still, they may remember it only selectively. The final picture they paint may be misleading, if not actually false. This is why a *corroboration of recollected evidence* is so very important. In other words, this material needs further supporting information from *other sources* before it can be effectively employed in a coursework assignment.

Support for fieldwork projects and further ideas on them may be found in a useful series entitled *Fieldwork Studies for Schools*. Each booklet in the seven-volume series contains twenty or thirty suggestions for possible fieldwork in a given area of the country, and is strong in social and economic topics. Even if the suggestions are in themselves unsuitable, they may well spark off some linked ideas for coursework with more direct bearing on your specific course.

2.5 History games and computer programs

Going electronic

A little thought will show you that as historical *evidence*, neither games nor computer programs are of quite the same order as the sources discussed above. Although they may be based on primary sources, both are in reality *manipulative techniques*. However, they are still valuable and important, and therefore ought to be included in this survey.

Before attempting to use either history games or computer programs in coursework assignments in Social and Economic History, you should make sure what use is permitted to be made of them within the framework of the examination. Even if your teacher does not know the answer to this question, the Exam Groups will certainly offer guidance to candidates on the matter. It would be foolish to employ either of them widely, only to discover in the end that the regulations of the examination did not permit their use. The basic rule will probably be that they are permitted, so long as they do not encroach on the *individual* character of the examination; i.e. what you offer for assessment in the examination must be your *own work* and not teamwork. This will probably have the effect of ruling out many of the games.

HISTORY GAMES

A number of publishers, such as Longman, now produce a number of these history games or *simulations* as they are often called because they simulate real historical situations. Broadly, such games reproduce the main features of original historical situations. They create an opportunity for students to react to the problems that were actually faced at the time, and share in the decision-taking that went on in the period. In this way, students can view problems 'from the inside', and come to understand *why* the original participants in these decisions chose to act in the way they did. They can work out for themselves what the consequences would have been if the decisions taken had been different, and so create an alternative scenario, e.g. what might have happened if MacDonald had followed a different policy in 1931, and not formed a National government? Students' decisions, taken on the evaluation of the evidence and by a process of negotiation, create a deeper understanding of the process of decision-taking.

Examples of history games

One such game is called *Hill Railway*. This is a simulation based on the construction of the Canterbury-Whitstable railway in 1830. Details of the limitations of the technology of the 1820s are provided in students' leaflets, and are the basis of a railway planning exercise.

Another game puts students in the role of canal-builders at the time of the Industrial Revolution. It starts with a screen map of north-west England in 1770, and shows the early navigations. During the next fifty years rival companies each aim to build canals across the Pennines to link the growing textile and mining towns of Lancashire and Yorkshire with outlets to the coast. Students are helped to compare their own results with the three canals eventually built across the Pennines, and the many other abortive schemes which were proposed during the period of canal-building.

Many games naturally take the form of a *group activity*, and as such may not be admissible for assessment as a GCSE exercise. Nevertheless, those playing the games may gain useful insights about the relationship between *intention*, *motive* and *cause*, and come to understand that events are often the result of the interaction of several forces and rarely the result of a single decision. Each player will have his own 'aims' and 'rules' in the game, and each will be seeking to secure specific objectives. Playing out the game will teach students that the process of reaching a successful outcome is more complicated and difficult than they thought. The hypothetical alternatives show that no particular outcome can be predicted with any certainty. This lessens the temptation – so evident in inexperienced students – to be 'wise after the event'. Personal decision making and problems are less suited to much of the subject matter of social and economic history, but material does exist and the group experience is very useful if a suitable and appropriate exercise can be found.

CHAPTER TWO **METHODS FOR EXTRACTING INFORMATION**

COMPUTER PROGRAMS

Computer-assisted learning packs are also currently produced to help students of GCSE Social and Economic History. One such pack concerns the *Analysis of Data from Burial Registers*, and is a program for interpreting information from burial registers. It can be used to introduce students to methods of handling evidence in a statistical form. There is a facility by which students can enter their own data.

Another program relates to *Census Analysis*. This provides an introduction to the problems of handling historical evidence. It uses the results of the 1851 census to give a valuable insight into the lives of a whole community. Students can encode their own data, creating new files based on census returns from their own local area, so encouraging local research.

Programs also often provide a good deal of supporting printed material, so making possible what is known as 'off-screen' work. Like history games, computer programs cast the student in an *active role* as an investigator rather than as an observer; but unlike games, which are team experiences, computer programs are geared to the activities of *individual students*.

Computer programs are also increasingly being used for *extracting specific information from masses of statistical material*. Those which extract birth rates or family sizes from censuses of population statistics, for example, will save the student the drudgery of sifting through mountains of figures, without lessening the importance of the task in hand. The time is fast coming when computers will be widely employed for mechanical tasks of manipulating existing information, freeing the historian to make new discoveries.

In securing software material, students have to be careful that their hardware equipment is compatible with it. Most programs are available in a variety of versions, each suited to a particular type of computer, the BBC, Archimedes, IBM PC or the RM Nimbus. They are not, of course, interchangeable, but should be used only on the right type of machine. The school's computer teacher will give fuller advice on this topic.

UNIT 3 METHODS FOR EXTRACTING INFORMATION

Evaluation or assessment topics in GCSE Social and Economic History are mainly *knowledge-based*, as indeed are empathy assignments. The methods to be adopted in such enquiries depend to an extent on the source of the information on which that knowledge is based.

3.1 Books and newspapers

The extraction of information from books and newspapers depends upon careful reading and note-taking. It is a means of *extending* the information provided by your teacher in the course of normal lessons. You should be careful to adopt the same good note-taking technique as you do for the rest of the course.

- Keep your notes legible;
- write in ink to prevent rubbing or fading;
- make intelligent use of headings, sub-headings and abbreviations.

❝Extracting the information❞

Make sure that you list *all* the main points rather than developing just one or two of them in unnecessary detail. Pick out with particular care those points that are obviously *relevant* to the subject of your enquiry. Try not to generate too much of note material when you are embarking on a coursework project, especially not multiple accounts of the same event as it appears in different books. Try instead to slot your note material together, so that new information from later sources fits in neatly with the material you have built up already.

You may find that using different coloured inks or highlighting key words with a marker pen helps to make your notes easier to use. Some people write their notes on one side of the paper only, so that the opposite blank page can be used for additions later gathered from other texts. Notes may be arranged in the form of a diagram with linking arrows, or in tabular form, if this is more appropriate.

Books may be used several at a time. It is not essential that you should finish with one text before moving to the next. The useful thing about books and newspapers, of course, is that you can refer *back* to an earlier section if you find there is something you have forgotten or need to check again. The same is true of a tape recording, but you may find this less easy.

3.2 TV, sound broadcast and film

Unless you have the use of a video tape recorder, or unless you can actually run film through the projector again, the type of replay just mentioned is not available for other information media. You should therefore take rough notes as fast as you can during the programme, or, if it is too dark for that, as soon as possible afterwards, while the memory is still fresh in your mind. Where a recording device is being used, you may find there is a pause button which will enable you to produce good, thorough notes.

With broadcasts or with films, you may be watching or listening to the programme alone, or with the rest of the class. Conditions are likely to be more difficult with a group, but the compensation is that your teacher may well have worked out some way of helping you with the notes you have to make.

You may be asked to evaluate the programme's coverage of the subject. In this case it will be necessary for you to set it against the background of your other knowledge, so as to be able to comment on its usefulness. Your comments will not be of an artistic character, since your task is that of the historian and not of the art critic. Whereas other films or TV broadcasts are often seen in isolation from one another, this, to be useful, must be seen in its historical context.

3.3 Visits and field trips

There are no action replays in this kind of historical activity, and your notes must be taken *at the time*, or very *shortly afterwards*. A spirally-bound notebook may be the best thing for your notes in this case, so that you can easily move from page to page, and a pencil may be better than a pen. You may find that *sketches* of the things you are looking at, built up into labelled diagrams, will be the best way of recording what you need. Don't forget that some of these observations will be taken in the open air (or even in the rain), and that the fewer loose papers you have the better.

Some sites may provide *document packs* of information, and may even suggest questions for you to follow up. If printed materials can be taken home, you may be saved a good deal of the writing that you would otherwise have to do at the time.

Sites are also useful for the *empathetic experience* they can produce. It is easier to understand how a factory hand of the early nineteenth century felt, if your site visit has given you first hand experience of the conditions in which he worked and lived.

3.4 Documentary sources

❝ How to deal with the documents ❞

In most cases you will not select the pieces of evidence for yourself except possibly where it is local archival material relating to the project on which you are engaged. Normally, an exercise of this sort will be given you by your teacher, and your skills will be revealed in your answers to the teacher's questions. Some of the skills which will be measured are:

- comprehension and interpretation
- evaluation

COMPREHENSION

You must *know what the passages mean*. You must be familiar with their vocabulary, their sentence structure and their contemporary modes of expression. To assist you in comprehension, ordinary dictionaries are a help, at least as a starting point, with words such as 'puddling' and 'fiduciary'. A number of words, however, like 'relief' and 'enclosure', by their historical usage, have acquired almost a technical meaning. These may need to be verified before you are confident of the meaning of a passage. Some of the vocabulary may be in a different language such as French (like 'laissez-faire'), or it may contain abbreviations which need to be expanded and understood. You have to be sure that the *meaning* you attach to a word is not just the one we use now, but the meaning that would have been usual at the time. Even the word 'hopefully', which used to mean 'in an optimistic way', has in the last twenty years come to mean merely 'perhaps'. A passage may also contain difficult words conveying complicated concepts, such as 'stagflation', and you must understand the meaning of any such words.

INTERPRETATION

There is more to understanding than vocabulary. You must be able to grasp the author's intention in writing the passage and to appreciate its shades of meaning – whether it is humorous, dismissive, ironic or patronising. From the author's choice of words you have to be able to judge the passage's tone. You have to be able to see it in the context of the problem with which it is dealing. Cartoons, speeches, letters, and even official documents may all have subtle hidden meanings. Nevertheless, care is needed here. Once more, you have to be sure that the meaning you attach to a phrase is not anachronistic, but is the meaning that would have been usual at the time. The words 'liquidate' and 'liquidation' are economic terms from the vocabulary of bankruptcy, but make sure that they are not used in their political sense of 'killing' or 'massacre', as employed by some vicious dictator. Later still the word was used also as a synonym for the word 'resolve' or 'fulfil', as in the statement 'We have liquidated all the objectives of our forward economic planning'.

Other phrases may have been used in different ways by different people. 'Economic progress', when heard from the mouth of an early nineteenth century industrialist, would have quite a different ring when heard from a member of the new Labour government in 1945. Similarly, 'the rights of the rank-and-file trade union members' sound quite different when applied to the strikers of 1926 than they do when the words are used by a Conservative politician of the 1980s. Thus *interpretation* goes further than vocabulary in revealing your grasp of a historical situation.

EVALUATION

You need not only to understand the passages quoted, you must also be able to *weigh them up*. You have to ask yourself about:

▶ **Authenticity**. Is the document you are using genuine, or is it a *fake*? In some cases a document contains an obvious error that marks it down as spurious, but in other cases its origin is more doubtful, and has to be decided on the basis of probability.

▶ **Reliability**. Can we be sure that the document is truthful in what it says? It may be that the author of the document was misinformed, or that he was prejudiced; perhaps he was simply lying. For a variety of reasons, it may be that we cannot put as much trust in the document as we would like. Even official statistics should be regarded with some scepticism. Governments may have a vested interest in editing and selecting them, and they may differ widely from statistics from other sources which may themselves be suspect for different reasons. Statistics from the eighteenth century or earlier may be unreliable simply because *accurate* figures are unobtainable. If you use such data you should check how they have been arrived at – most reliable sources of such statistics will give some indication of this – and then you can add your own cautionary comment.

▶ **Validity**. Does the document prove what it is *supposed* to prove, or is it being used mistakenly to attempt to support a misleading or inaccurate idea? For example, are all the statements of the Anti-Corn Law League proof of the 'evils' of the Corn Laws, or are all the statements of the *British Gazette* in 1926 proof that the strikers were trying to overthrow the British Constitution?

In other words, there are three questions we should ask of any historical document:

1 Is it genuine?
2 Is it truthful?
3 Is it logically sound?

Please note that the answer to the first of these questions is quite scientific, and will take the form of a straightforward yes or no. However, the answers to the other two are more subjective, and allow difference of opinion.

In addition you have to be able to show your mastery of:

▶ **Analysis**. You have to be able to look at the component units of a document and see how it works, and how it achieves its effect. You have to be able to use the document to comment on the ideas of similarity and difference, change and continuity, and cause and consequence, any of which may be illustrated by it. You have to be able to decide whether it is sensible and closely argued, or whether it is wild and far-fetched. You have to be able to deduce the extent to which it fits closely with another document, or is at variance with it.

▶ **Bias**. You have to be able to detect bias, whether it occurs deliberately, as it usually does, or whether it occurs naturally and unconsciously. Bias must be distinguished from both *opinion* and *judgment*. In the last two cases, the writer of the document is prepared to offer reasons for the view he takes, dissociating it from his personal emotions. But in the case of bias, he offers no reasons for his view, and presumes that naturally everyone else will share his assumptions. He frequently becomes heated and emotionally involved in the stance he thinks to be proper, and fails to deal fairly with opinions contradicting his own. Unconscious bias is very difficult to deal with, since it may not be easy to detect, especially when a sympathetic reader or audience shares the author's views.

- **Inconsistency**. Documents may contain contradictions, or differing statements which cannot easily be reconciled with one another. You have to be able to *identify* these, and attempt to *explain* them. Sometimes the case is a simple one, as with figures in a table which fail to add up; in other cases the inconsistency (where it exists) is more subtle and needs more lengthy explanation. A supporter of the government in 1834, for example, might declare that the government is not hostile to trade unions as such, but that the Tolpuddle labourers have been convicted for their *criminal* activities.

- **Gaps**. These are particularly important in statistics, and social and economic historians derive many of their conclusions from interpreting statistics. It is vital, therefore, that you should notice when statistics are *missing* from a table, when trends have been *distorted* by deliberate choice of the initial or final years (e.g. price statistics from 1921 to 1933 would show no inflation at all, but marked deflation – this may have been intended as part proof of a shaky argument). Also, when major factors of direct bearing are omitted (e.g. changing money values from wage statistics to illustrate poverty). This is in addition to looking at the origin and authenticity of the statistics. You have to be able to detect omissions in statistics and other types of source, and to comment on the possible explanations of the omission. Where an explanation is offered, you have to be able to say whether, in your opinion, it is adequate.

- **Extrapolations**. You have to make intelligent efforts to fill in any gaps that may exist in the evidence. For instance, if you were informed that in 1901 the population of Great Britain was 37 million and in 1911 it was 41 million, you might reasonably suppose that in 1906 it was somewhere between the two. But beware of *assuming* that, because the date was the exact halfway point between 1901 and 1911, the population increase by 1906 would also be the exact halfway point between the two figures. There are further limitations to the sort of extrapolations that can properly be made. Mark Twain, in 1874, had perhaps the last word to say on the subject:

  In the space of 176 years the Lower Mississippi has shortened itself 242 miles. That is, an average of a trifle of a mile and a third per year. Therefore, any calm person, who is not blind or idiotic, can see that in the Silurian period, just a million years ago next November, the Lower Mississippi was upward of 1,300,000 miles long, and stuck out over the Gulf of Mexico like a fishing rod. And by the same token anyone can see that 742 years from now the Lower Mississippi will be only a mile and three-quarters long, and Cairo (USA) and New Orleans will have joined their streets together, and be plodding comfortably along under a single mayor and a mutual board of aldermen. There is something fascinating about science.

- **Comparisons**. You should be able to compare two documents from the point of view of tone and factual content (see pages 16–17).

RESEARCH AND INVESTIGATION

The methods of investigation in all these types of documentary assignment are very similar. In the case of documents you have selected for yourself, they should illustrate the particular points which you wish them to demonstrate. In all other cases you should take care to:

1. **Read and study the document closely.** Close study is just as necessary with non-verbal material (photographs, engravings, statistics) as it is with verbal extracts. Graphs and tables must be studied particularly closely, you cannot answer detailed questions unless you are thoroughly familiar with the contents.

2. **Note the 'attribution' provided for each document.** You should be provided with the *name* of the author, the *date* of the extract and the *source* from which it is taken. The same is true of non-verbal material, e.g. engravings and photographs, which may have the name of the source, the date, and possibly a caption. In the case of cartoons, the name of the cartoonist will be included. Tables and graphs should also acknowledge their sources. You should note these carefully, since you may need to make use of this information when you assess the reliability or validity of a source in the course of your answer.

3. **Read the questions set on the sources carefully.** Make sure that you have properly understood the questions before attempting your answer. In particular, check that you can answer *every* part of the question – do not be deceived by one or two easy 'openers' into thinking that the whole question is easy.

4. **Use the mark allocation as a guide to the length of answer.** If a *mark tariff* is provided with the question, use this as a guide for how much you should write. If only 1 mark is on offer, a one-word or a one-phrase answer will be adequate; anything more would be a waste of time. But if 6 or 8 marks are on offer, you will need to write more fully

and to make a number of relevant points, so that you have a chance of reaching the maximum.

5 **Plan your answers for all parts of the assignment**. Work out roughly in your head the sort of material you ought to use in answering each sub-question. There is nothing worse than finding that you have 'over-written' an earlier answer, and have to repeat yourself in a later one. Putting 'ditto', or 'see a)ii) above' looks like lack of planning on your part.

6 **Make specific use of the document in your answer**. If the question says 'Refer to the document ...' or 'Use the document to show ...' then make *specific use* of the document in your answer, quoting short passages as appropriate. Above all, do not ignore the document and avoid the mistake of relying on your memory to give the answer you think the question ought to have.

7 **Use short quotations from the document**. You could also, of course, quote figures from the source to illustrate your points. Do not copy out documents or quote figures at length. If you use a quotation, indicate in your answer the point which it is meant to illustrate, e.g. the author's bias, sarcasm, ambiguity, etc. Use quotation marks to indicate your quotation. Instead of copying out a quotation, line-number references may be used instead.

CHAPTER 3

USING STATISTICS AND EVIDENCE MATERIAL

In doing coursework assignments, students of social and economic history must be prepared to make extensive use of *evidence*, especially evidence of a statistical nature. They must also be ready to use maps, photographs and even cartoons relating to the subject. Unfortunately, GCSE students do not always use their evidence to the best effect, even though there is a general assumption that they ought to know how. This chapter is designed to help to improve their performance.

> " Use your evidence wisely "

UNIT 1   MAPS AND ILLUSTRATIONS

1.1 Maps

Maps have a particular value in social and economic history, and can be used in assignment work to very good effect. If you are using existing maps for tracing or photocopying, you should first of all select the most directly useful and relevant maps. Remember that the map is there to *convey information*, and not simply to act as decoration to improve the look of your work. Black and white maps are normally better than coloured ones, in that they often convey this information more crisply.

USING MAPS

When using a map that is already drawn, you must make sure that the basic requirements are fulfilled:

a) You should be sure that the map includes a *north pointer*. This is to prevent you from reproducing the map upside-down, and at the same time to ensure that anyone using it can immediately see the direction of the surrounding features of the map from the main subject-matter which it illustrates. If there is no north pointer on the map, you should insert one.

b) You have to know the *scale* of the map. If you have two maps to show the railway networks of, for example, Britain and the USA, it is important to show the two scales, or otherwise you may draw some very mistaken conclusions. Whatever it may look like on the map, the distance from London to Bristol, for instance, is less than 150 miles, but that from Richmond (Virginia) to Los Angeles is over 2500 miles – about sixteen times further! If your map does not provide a scale, it is a good idea to work one out and include it.

c) You have to remember that different map projections give different apparent land sizes, and even shapes. The Mercator projection, for example, has the effect of making Greenland and Africa look quite similar in size, when in fact Africa is many times bigger, with 11,700,000 square miles as against Greenland's 840,000. You must be careful, once again, not to draw conclusions from what the maps *look like* – rather, from what they *are*.

INFORMATION FROM MAPS

Maps may contain, of course, a great deal of information relevant to the subject being studied apart from purely geographical information. Study the map in Figure 3.1 on the population of England and Wales in 1701. You will see that we are told that England was predominantly an agricultural country; that Bristol was the second city in England; that Birmingham, Liverpool and Manchester were new towns, and that there was an important centre of the woollen industry in Norfolk. Select five other pieces of information which are given to you which you

CHAPTER THREE **MAPS AND ILLUSTRATIONS**

would not be able to find out from an ordinary map. You may also find shortcomings in this map – apart from the obvious lack of a *scale* and of a *north pointer*. You may regret, for instance, that the map does not inform us what the *total population* of England and Wales was at this time. Can you find any more? N.B. You ought *not* to fault the map for not providing information it is not designed to provide – e.g. it contains no information about Scotland, nor does it tell us about exports and imports.

POPULATION 1701
England was predominantly an agricultural country. The most densely populated parts were the most prosperous agricultural regions. There were no great industrial conurbations.

The six northern counties contained less than one-fifth of the total population.

A poor, barren, isolated district with few roads and few people.

York – 10000 – had doubled its size since the time of Domesday Book.

Liverpool Manchester

Norwich, the centre of the woollens manufacturing district of East Anglia, was the third city of England.

Wrexham (Bersham)

New towns in the North and Midlands were beginning to grow rapidly.

The small population of Wales increased with the development of the iron industry.

Birmingham

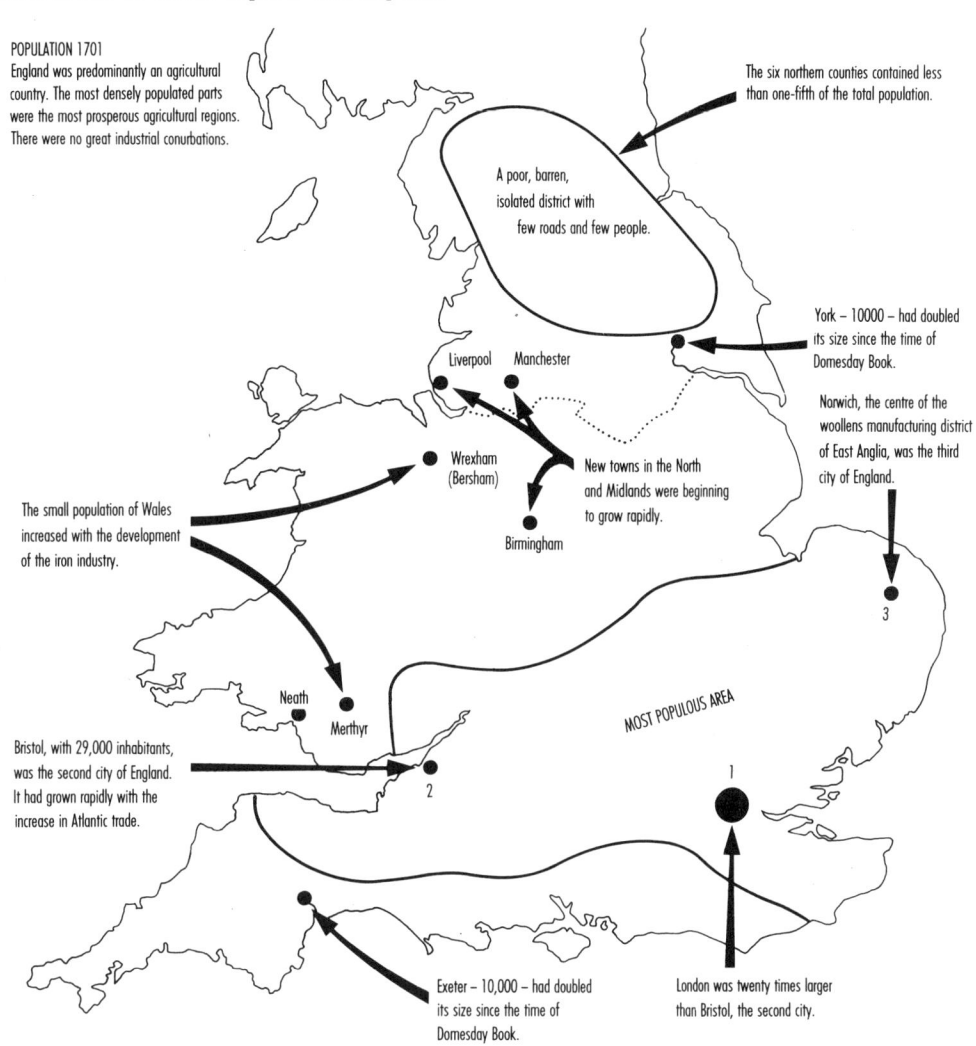

Neath
Merthyr

MOST POPULOUS AREA

Bristol, with 29,000 inhabitants, was the second city of England. It had grown rapidly with the increase in Atlantic trade.

Exeter – 10,000 – had doubled its size since the time of Domesday Book.

London was twenty times larger than Bristol, the second city.

Fig 3.1
Information from maps

MAPS AND DIAGRAMS

Maps may also be used diagrammatically to convey information not normally associated with map presentation. Not all the information conveyed may be ideally suited to maps, but they may nonetheless have the advantage of putting together a mass of relevant information in a convenient form, saving a rather cumbersome textual presentation. The map in Figure 3.2, on the subject of the Great Agricultural Depression in Britain, uses a map, but combines this with a number of other useful features. It tells us, for instance about the relative effects of the Depression on wheat production and on fruit growing. Can you find two other sorts of information which are provided?

DIAGRAMS

Diagrams are also valuable in social and economic history for much the same reasons. They should not be seen as a form of ornamentation, but as a convenient way of presenting detailed information without a lot of textual coverage. They may, as in Figure 3.3, take the form of a 'flow diagram', thus revealing in an economical way the *relationship* between different stages of iron and steel production. This information may be combined with other information taking different forms, as with the two bar-charts and the graph in this case. (There is more information about these types of diagrams later in this chapter.) Can you find two or three examples of useful information which this diagram provides? Or one or two weaknesses in the diagram? You may, for instance, find it unfortunate that no *units* are provided in the two bar-charts at the bottom of the diagram.

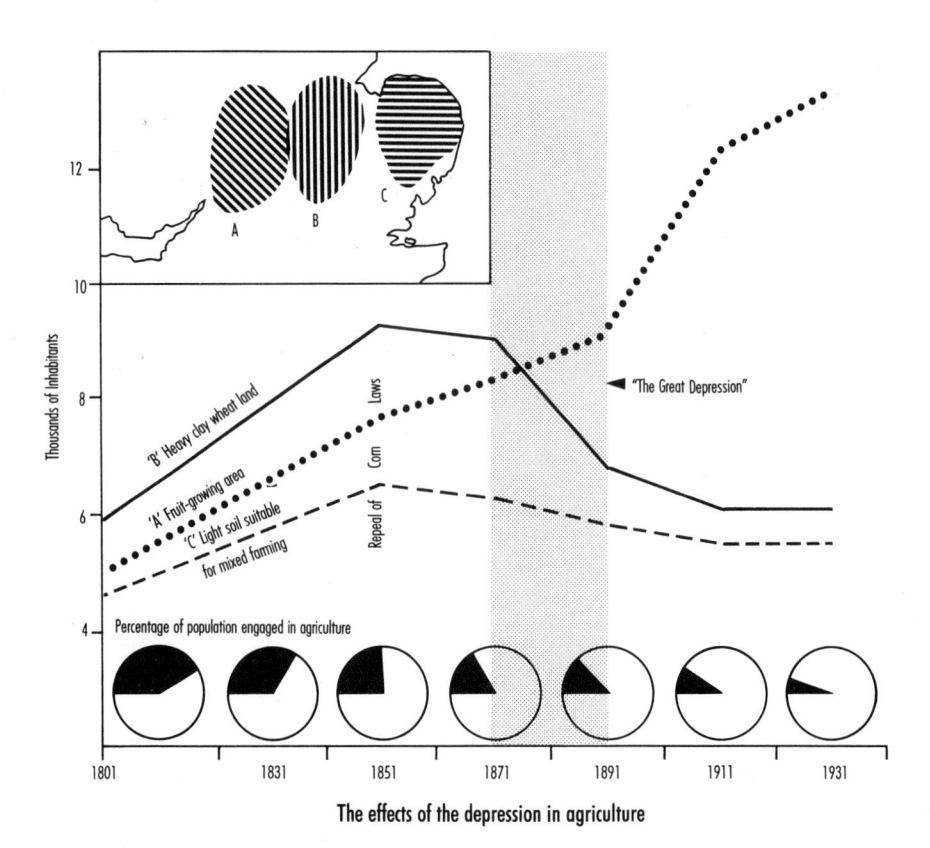

CHAPTER THREE USING STATISTICS AND EVIDENCE MATERIAL

Fig 3.2
Maps and diagrams

The effects of the depression in agriculture

❝ Should I copy my maps? ❞

Before you trace or photocopy maps or diagrams which you have found in books, you should first discuss the matter with your teacher. Many teachers and examiners hold the opinion that using material borrowed from other people's books is little better than copying their words, and that either process results in the presentation of work that is not really your own. The GCSE examination is intended to discourage what are sometimes called 'scissors-and-paste'

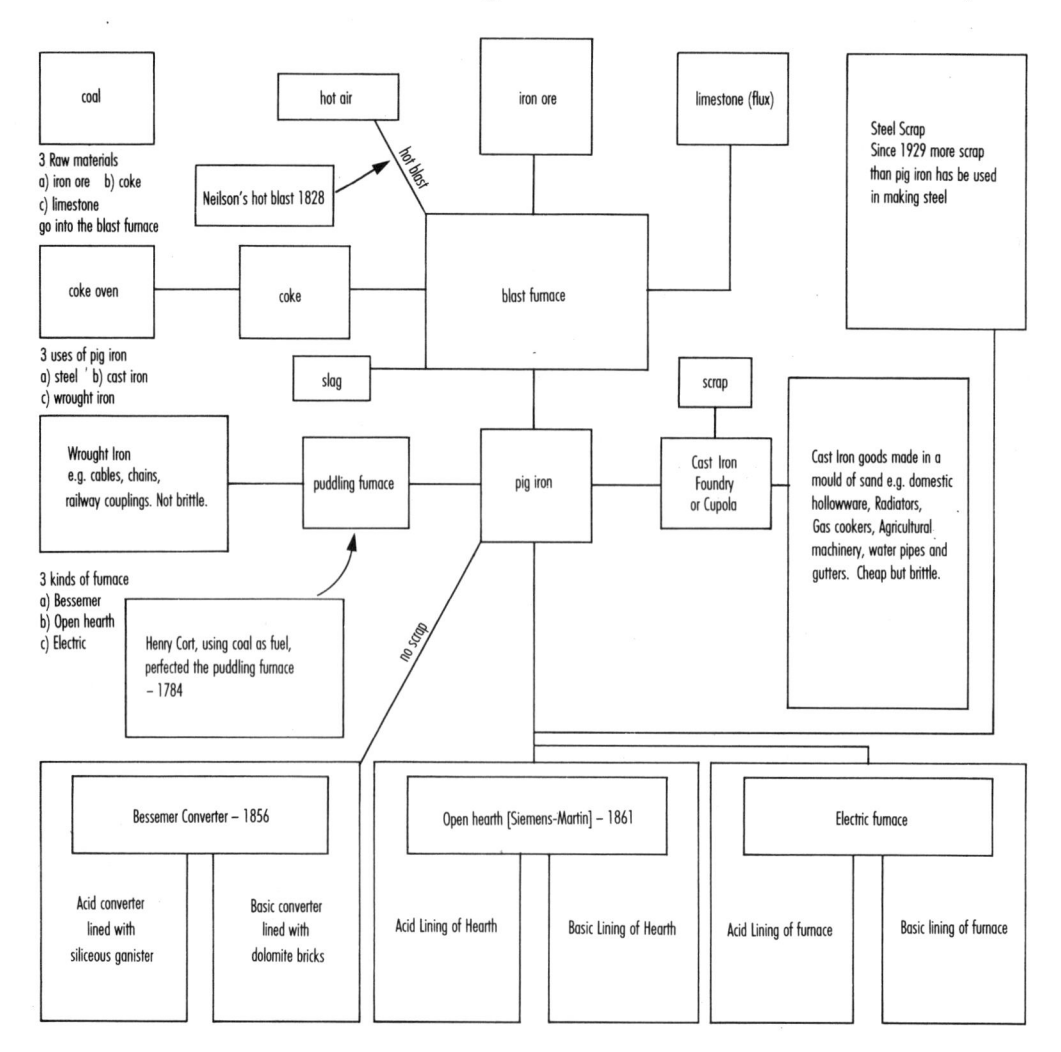

CHAPTER THREE MAPS AND ILLUSTRATIONS   37

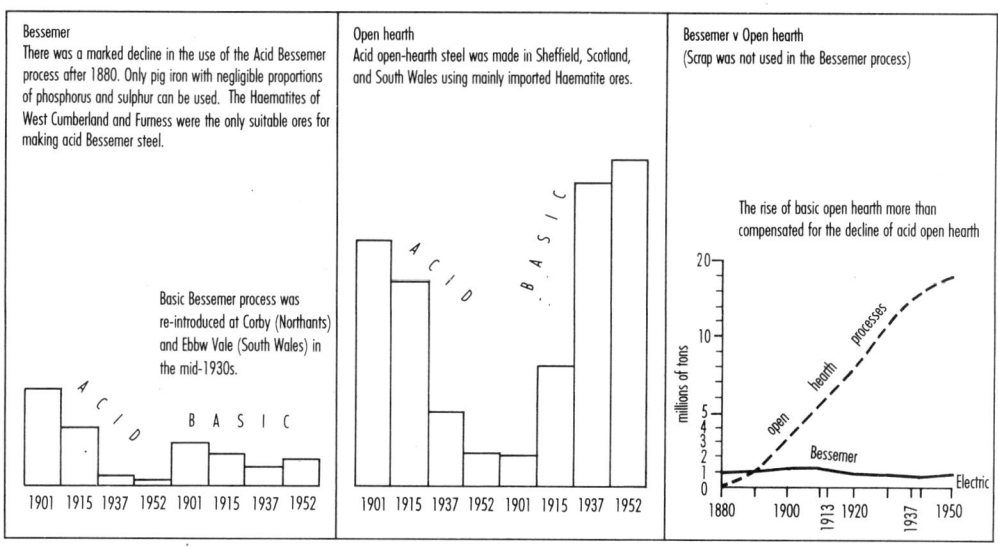

Bessemer
There was a marked decline in the use of the Acid Bessemer process after 1880. Only pig iron with negligible proportions of phosphorus and sulphur can be used. The Haematites of West Cumberland and Furness were the only suitable ores for making acid Bessemer steel.

Basic Bessemer process was re-introduced at Corby (Northants) and Ebbw Vale (South Wales) in the mid-1930s.

Open hearth
Acid open-hearth steel was made in Sheffield, Scotland, and South Wales using mainly imported Haematite ores.

Bessemer v Open hearth
(Scrap was not used in the Bessemer process)

The rise of basic open hearth more than compensated for the decline of acid open hearth

Fig 3.3
Diagrams

Methods of making iron and steel

methods, by which students patch together snippets of information lifted from a variety of sources, passing off the results as their own work. The examination is not meant to test the accuracy with which you can copy out the work of others, but your own historical skills in locating and independently employing relevant information.

Constructing diagrams and maps

Constructing your own diagrams, however, and building up your own maps – perhaps even combining the two – demands a range of skills higher than those associated with GCSE. Even the few instances we have seen so far are the results of the work of professional artists and cartographers, and you, without any formal training, cannot be expected to be as good as they are. What is acceptable is for you to *borrow* some of their ideas, but to combine them with ideas of your own. You can show that you have mastered skills of *translation*, i.e. expressing the same ideas in a different form, or of *collation*, i.e. bringing together different information from different sources and putting it side by side. This process is actually much superior to merely making a copy. For one thing, copying does not reveal any understanding, whereas the process described certainly does. For another, editing your information in your own presentation enables you to omit the less important information in favour of other information which may not originally have been included. If you are constructing your own maps and diagrams, you must remember:

❝Points to note about maps❞

a) In the case of *maps*, you must be sure that your outline is basically *accurate*, and that you have supplied a *north pointer* and a *scale* for the map. Students sometimes produce maps which are unnecessarily elaborate and complicated, with quantities of irrelevant information included. However, the reverse is often true; the map outline is so badly drawn as to be unrecognizable, or else there are basic omissions from the information. It is not easy to draw a map of England, nor of other countries which may be less familiar in their outline. Some maps of England are so distorted as to be incapable of accurate use – a roughly circular squiggle, with assorted capes and estuaries, bearing so little resemblance to the original as to invalidate any useful information that otherwise it might include.

b) In the case of *diagrams*, you should be careful to label the axes in a graph, or to provide units for bar charts and for tables. Dates, percentages, etc. should be carefully labelled. To save yourself the trouble of putting 'million' or 'thousand' every time, you can put at the head of the diagram that it is 'millions' or 'thousands'. It is perfectly permissible to use clear abbreviations – 000 for thousands, m for millions, £ for pounds, and so on. In the case of a percentage, % is quite acceptable. Remember that your objective is to combine brevity with accuracy.

Maps and diagrams may, of course, be supplied together with other information – a document, a table of statistics, a photograph etc. – in the form of an exercise which asks you to employ different sorts of information. In these cases you have the easier task of using information which someone else has supplied, but you have nevertheless to demonstrate historical skills in a different way. Examples of this are given later in this chapter.

1.2 Illustrations

PHOTOGRAPHS

These provide a good way of making the impact of your work more vivid and immediate, especially if they are well-chosen. Photographs should also be capable of crisp photocopying. Unfortunately, too many assignments are spoilt by poor photographs, either because they are in soft focus or else in colour, neither of which is a feature which photocopies effectively. Perhaps the best way of knowing whether the photographs you have chosen are suitable is by *trying to photocopy* them. If the result is poor, it is best to choose others, since not even the more efficient machines are capable of making much difference in final quality.

❝ Choice of photographs ❞

Choosing photographs

You should choose your photographs not purely on account of their dramatic qualities, but because they will *highlight* some point in your text by using their visual qualities. If, for example, you are writing about the British labour movement before 1914, and its attitude towards the First World War, a photograph like that in Figure 3.4 will make a powerful point. Of course, the photograph does not show that the bulk of the British working class was opposed to the war, but it nonetheless shows that Keir Hardie could attract an audience for his views – and his police guard also shows that in 1914 people were free to express opinions which may not have been to the liking of the ruling classes. Perhaps there are other social comments which you may be able to make as a result of observing the evidence visible in the photograph.

Fig 3.4

Again, a photograph such as the one in Figure 3.5 would be very helpful if you were writing about living conditions persisting even in recent times. It is a picture of a slum house in Newcastle in 1955, where five people lived in a single room. Overcrowding is one obvious feature. You might also like to comment on its poor lighting, its squalid untidiness, its open-fire heating, its few scraps of food permanently on the table, the strings of washing indoors and so on. Your text could then tie in these points with the welfare state conditions supposed to prevail at the time, and hint at the broad gap between political theory and actual reality.

Photographs should always be selected with great care so as to give a truthful account of what they depict. In choosing them, you should be cautious about accepting the old adage that 'the camera cannot lie'. It does, of course, portray the visual truth of the moment, but it may have been taken at a moment that was entirely untypical of the whole event. The photograph of Keir Hardie (Fig 3.4), for example, addressing a large group of the public in Trafalgar Square in conditions of calm and discipline, may have been taken only moments before a major riot broke out. The photograph would still be *true*, but could be said to be *misleading*. Furthermore, photographs can give us fictitious evidence. Scenes can be fabricated and posed by professional actors in appropriate costume. Because the scene has been captured on a photographic plate does not mean to say that it is true. Finally, photographs can be tampered with. Negatives can be edited by those sufficiently skilled to give a quite different false picture. People can be edited out, as though they were never on the scene at all; other people can be introduced, as if they were. Unwelcome bits of the picture can be removed, and appearances can be 'touched up' by the artist to look different.

Fig 3.5

> ... and
> engravings

ENGRAVINGS

These have many of the same virtues as photographs, but generally date from a time before cameras existed, or before they were in widespread use. If they date from a source contemporary with the scene they depict, they may be extremely valuable. For instance, if you are working on an assignment to do with the history of education in the nineteenth century, you may find it useful to include an engraving showing a monitorial school, such as the one in Figure 3.6. This gives a good idea of the school's internal appearance, its layout, the number of pupils handled, the use of pupil-teachers (or monitors), and so on. These and other points could tie in with your text and illustrate it well.

Fig 3.6

It is sometimes said that an engraving is *less truthful* than a photograph because the engraver chooses what to include and what to leave out when he is actually making the engraving. He may have exaggerated, for instance, the number of pupils in the school; or he may have left out a feature which he decided it was not appropriate to include – the number of windows in the roof, or the amount of litter on the floor. He may have created a false impression: is it a coincidence, for example, that he dresses all his little boys alike, when in fact they were in a variety of garbs, or is he telling us that pupils in a monitorial school wore some kind of uniform? His may be a rather glamourized view, or it may be over-critical. A moment's thought, however, will reveal that a photograph may be equally misleading or inappropriate. The cameraman, by choosing which scene to photograph and by arranging it and lighting it suitably, turns out to be just as responsible for editing his work as does the engraver. He may even have doctored the negative, or touched up the final print! You must bear in mind that *all* evidence of this sort, whether in a photograph, a painting, an engraving, a wood-cut, and so on, bears the imprint of the witness. In other words, the presentation of the evidence affects the nature of the testimony.

CARTOONS

Use of cartoons

Apart from their obvious use in examination papers, cartoons can provide excellent illustrations for your assignment work. They often manage to put over their message pithily, and are frequently amusing. They can express ideas pictorially which are too brutal or too impolite to go into words – if you were to say out loud some of the things they suggest in pictures, you would probably find yourself in court on a charge of slander! Or they may make their impact through the starkness, even the horror of their theme. Let us take two examples.

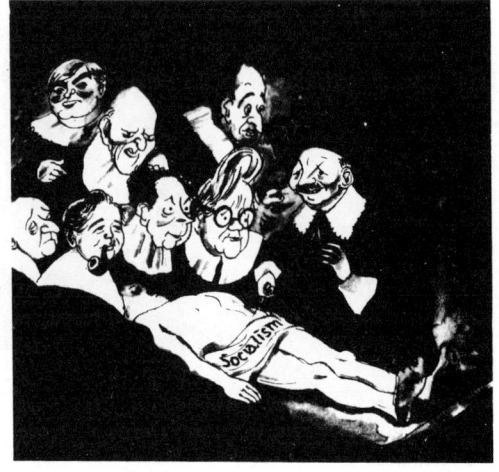

Fig 3.7

Fig 3.8

The first (Fig 3.7) is a *Punch* cartoon dating from 1858. It reveals the intense concern expressed by Londoners at that time for the purity of their water supplies. In those days, the city's sewers and street drains poured sewage and filth into the Thames at an alarming rate, whilst at the same time Londoners drew their drinking water from the same river. The result was the ever-present danger of diseases such as cholera and typhoid, both of them infections aggravated by dirty water and inadequate sewage disposal. *Punch* showed its alarm by depicting disease as a sinister figure rowing on the river and surrounded by vegetation and the floating carcasses of dead animals thrown into the water. Disease is portrayed as a shrouded skeleton, half-turned towards us as it paddles past in its little skiff. The caption – 'Your money our your life' (the phrase traditionally employed by highwaymen) – suggests that there is a choice between cleaning up London's river, which will certainly be an expensive business, and remaining idle whilst large number of people perish. There is no humour in this cartoon; only a grim awareness of the ugly reality.

The second cartoon (Fig 3.8) is much more obviously satirical in its intent. The cartoonist was Vicky, a refugee immigrant from continental Europe to Britain during the 1930s, a confirmed socialist who doubted the genuine socialist credentials of the Attlee cabinet in the post-war period. The figures in the portrait are shown in seventeenth-century costume with wide, white lace collars over their sombre garments. One of them, Attlee himself, wears a broad-brimmed black hat. The cartoon echoes Rembrandt's famous portrayal of *The Anatomy Lesson*, showing a group of eminent Netherlands surgeons grouped around a cadaver, with their leader beginning the dissection. If you are sufficiently familiar with faces, you will see, in addition to Attlee, Herbert Morrison with his famous quiff of hair, next to him Hugh Gaitskell, with pointed nose and frizzy hair, and next to him a youthful and cherubic Harold Wilson smoking his pipe. All the caricatures are rather cruel. A nice touch of irony is that Nye Bevan, the main architect of the famous National Health Service, is tucked away in the background and not directly involved in the 'operation'. The lampoon is not entirely good-natured. The message would seem to be that this bunch of characters knew even less about socialism than the Dutch doctors knew about surgery.

USING ILLUSTRATIONS

Illustrations, of course, may be supplied with other information – a document, a table of statistics, a map, etc. – in the form of an exercise which asks you to employ several sorts of historical skills. In such cases you do not have to select the information for yourself, but you have the task of demonstrating our skills in a different way. Take the following example of this extract, written by a Headmaster in 1952, and describing the change that had taken place over three generations of pupils:

CHAPTER THREE **MAPS AND ILLUSTRATIONS**   41

The boy of 1900 as compared with the boy of 1880. Much more docile; insubordination now almost unknown. Cheerful and eager now – then, often sullen and morose. All this, the result of discipline and control at school; reacts beneficially at home. Personal cleanliness – greatly improved: verminous cases among boys rare, but among girls almost universal, due to their long hair. As to dirt, it is necessary to distinguish between recent dirt got at play, and the ancient kind that gives the strong smell. The vermin referred to are lice; bugs are rarely seen; but fleas are common, especially on children coming from homes where there is a baby.

❝ **Study this example** ❞

Fig 3.9

What is important here is that you thoroughly examine the evidence. Producing answers to the questions asked from your own recollection, and *ignoring* what the evidence contains, is no way to secure a good mark in the exercise, any more than *contradicting* the evidence because it appears to go against your own cherished ideas on the subject, or against something you remember being taught.

Look carefully, for example, at the three photographs in Figure 3.9. What changes can you see taking place in the intervals of years between their being taken? Study the expressions on the faces of the schoolchildren. Is there a bigger contrast between the first and the second photographs, or between the second and the third? How would you describe the expressions on the faces of the children in the photographs – which faces seem the most pleasant, which the most familiar, which the most varied, etc? Look at the backgrounds to the three photographs (as far as they are visible). What does it tell us about the school buildings which they attended? Do you notice the change from an asphalt yard to a grass playing-field? Look at the costumes the schoolchildren are wearing. What can you learn from them? Even the fact that only one of the photographs includes girls may be said to be significant. Why is that?

The extract is interesting enough in itself. It gains some authority by its authorship. If it had been written by a solicitor, or by a refuse collector, we might attach less weight to it – but to be written by a headmaster means that it is more directly from the source. It tells us, too, what headmasters think: what they *expect* of their children, and the things that to them are *important*. You will see the close attention he pays to *personal cleanliness*, to *dirt*, to *smell* and to *vermin*. The extract, in fact, is almost as informative on the subject of *headmasters* as it is on the subject of *schoolchildren*.

Questions may be asked also comparing the two types of sources, photographic and documentary. How far can we say that one bears out the other? How appropriate are the words used by the headmaster 'sullen and morose' and 'cheerful and eager'? Would you say that one sort of evidence broadly *corroborates* the other, or *contradicts* it?

CHAPTER THREE   USING STATISTICS AND EVIDENCE MATERIAL

UNIT 2 THE USE OF STATISTICAL MATERIAL

Statistical information is very valuable in Social and Economic History

In social and economic history, *statistical evidence* provides an important source of information, and you have to learn to use it properly. If you are referring to road or canal construction, to state expenditure on education or on workhouses, or to birth and death rates, you ought to be able to bring out the figures to prove the point you are trying to make. Generalizations that are not supported by the necessary evidence may invite disbelief, for there are limits on what you can ask people to accept on trust. On the other hand, if you wish to employ statistics to prove your point, you must do it properly.

Statistical information may be expressed in various ways, in the form of tables, graphs and diagrams, to name only the most common. All of these may be used in your coursework, and the information deriving from one source may often be usefully *translated* into another.

(1) Tables

2.1 Statistical tables

Tables may be used to express a mass of useful information extremely *concisely*. Let us take the table in Figure 3.10 as an example. If you are to use figures of this sort accurately you have first to understand the *terminology*. It is necessary to know what ingots and castings *are*, the differences between the Bessemer and the Open Hearth processes, the differences between acid steel and basic steel and the differences in their production. There should be at least some discussion of these in your text, unless your comments are to be meaningless.

You have also to know what *percentages* are in arithmetic, and what *averages* are. A term used in this table is a *quinquennial average*, that is, the average of the individual figures for five successive years, so as to remove the erratic variations that may occur from year to year. Where entries are for *individual* years, the relevant date is attached in brackets. It is worth noting, too, that the use of a dash, i.e. '–', means that the figures are insignificantly small, or that they are irrelevant, or even that we ought to include them, but we do not know what they are. Please distinguish a dash ('–') from a zero ('0'). Zero, of course, means *nothing*, i.e. that in a given year the production was *nought*. What does the use of dashes in columns 7 and 8 of this table mean? It may mean that before 1885 the acid and the basic processes were not known, or were not used. We know this to be false from consulting other sources. It therefore probably means that before 1885, though figures were kept, they were not broken down into acid and basic processes as they are later than that year.

Year	Total '000 tons	Bessemer '000 tons	Bessemer % total	Open Hearth '000 tons	Open Hearth % total	Acid Process %	Basic Process %
1871–4	486	444	91.3	42	8.7	–	–
1875–9	883	742	84	141	16	–	–
1880–4	1,793	1,402	78.1	391	21.9	–	–
1885–9	2,814	1,818	64.6	996	35.4	86 (1889)	14 (1889)
1890–4	3,143	1,637	51.8	1,506	48.2	86	14
1895–9	4,260	1,764	41.4	2,496	58.6	84	16
1900–4	4,955	1,774	36	3,181	64	79	21
1905–9	5,994	1,690	28	4,304	72	72	28
1910–14	7,007	1,529	22	5,478	78	73	27
1915–19	8,938	1,271	14	7,410	82	53	44
1920–4	7,067	556	8	6,414	91	37	62
1925–9	7,647	443	6	7,083	93	33	66
1930–4	6,733	195	3	6,409	95	25	73
1935–9	11,257	564	5	10,391	92	20	77

Fig 3.10
Steel output in the United Kingdom (ingots and castings)
Annual average for each quinquennium

You ought to be able to read this table. The first line, for example, means that in the four years from 1871 to 1874 (this appears to be the only line where the figures are *not* a quinquennial average), a total of 486 000 tons of steel were produced. Of this, 444 000 were made by the Bessemer process, and 42 000 by the Open Hearth process. In the first case, this was 91.3% of the total, and in the second 8.7%. It follows, therefore, that the figures in the third and fifth columns should add up to the total in the second column – and do; and that the figures in the fourth and sixth columns should add up to 100 – which they do (until 1915!).

Examiners might also expect you to be able to see in which five-year period the increase was the greatest, or to pick out from the table the occasions on which steel output fell, instead of increasing. They might expect you to be able to pick out the year in which the records were broken down into how much of the steel produced was acid steel, and how much basic. You might also be expected to use the figures to comment on the rise of the Open Hearth process, and the decline of the Bessemer converter.

CHAPTER THREE THE USE OF STATISTICAL MATERIAL

(2) Diagrams   **2.2** Statistical diagrams

PIE CHARTS

These are circles, divided into slices or segments, to show what size shares in a given quantity are taken up by various factors. e.g. what proportions of various EEC nationals visit Swiss holiday resorts in a year. Statistically, they may not be very accurate, since it is difficult to draw a segment representing exactly 17.4% – and just as difficult to quantify it from the diagram, unless you have a protractor. The pie chart's main strength, however, is that it gives a good idea of the *relative* or *proportionate* sizes of shares in a given whole.

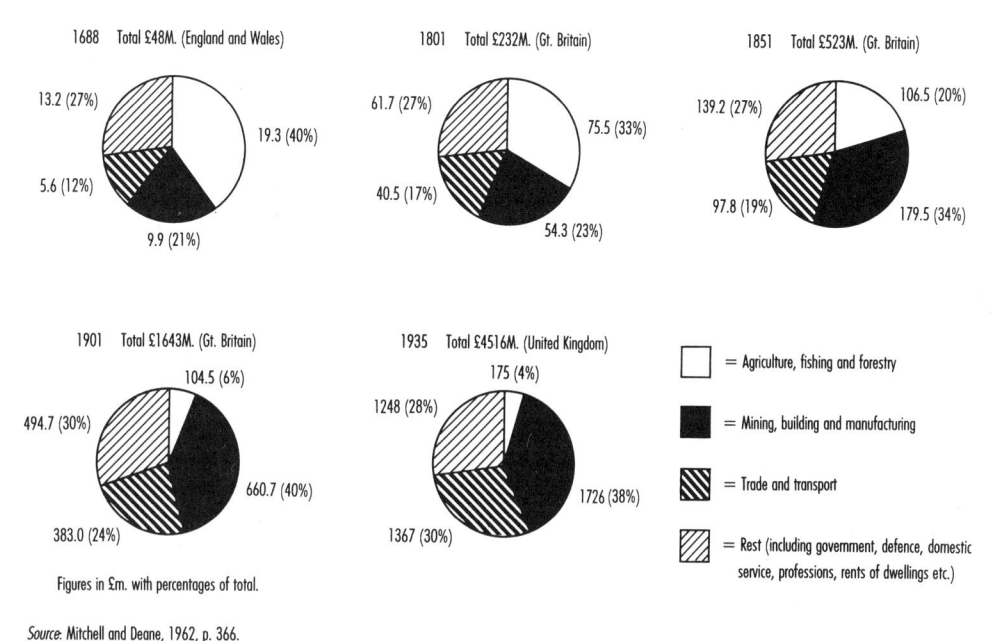

1688   Total £48M. (England and Wales)
- 13.2 (27%)
- 19.3 (40%)
- 5.6 (12%)
- 9.9 (21%)

1801   Total £232M. (Gt. Britain)
- 61.7 (27%)
- 75.5 (33%)
- 40.5 (17%)
- 54.3 (23%)

1851   Total £523M. (Gt. Britain)
- 139.2 (27%)
- 106.5 (20%)
- 97.8 (19%)
- 179.5 (34%)

1901   Total £1643M. (Gt. Britain)
- 104.5 (6%)
- 494.7 (30%)
- 660.7 (40%)
- 383.0 (24%)

1935   Total £4516M. (United Kingdom)
- 175 (4%)
- 1248 (28%)
- 1726 (38%)
- 1367 (30%)

Key:
- ☐ = Agriculture, fishing and forestry
- ■ = Mining, building and manufacturing
- ▨ = Trade and transport
- ▧ = Rest (including government, defence, domestic service, professions, rents of dwellings etc.)

Fig 3.11
Pie charts: National income; shares of national income by industrial sectors

Figures in £m. with percentages of total.

Source: Mitchell and Deane, 1962, p. 366.

Examine the pie chart in Figure 3.11. You will see from this example the absolute importance of attaching an explanatory key. For a black-and-white presentation (the usual one) you will therefore need distinctive varieties of shading, so that the diagram is easy to decipher. The figures attached to the various segments *quantify* the sizes of the shares, and avoid the criticism made above that pie diagrams are imprecise (though the use of the figures tends to make the pie diagram itself unnecessary).

The pie-chart in Figure 3.11 illustrates admirably the growth of the manufacturing sector of the British economy since the end of the seventeenth century. In 1688, we see that this sector accounted for 21% of the total economy of England and Wales; by 1935 – this time for Great Britain – it had grown to 38%. It is true that the basis of comparison is not the same – it shifts from England and Wales to Great Britain (and after 1800 includes Ireland), and finishes with the United Kingdom, i.e. of Great Britain and Northern Ireland. This variation introduces another, and rather unwelcome, variable into the problem, but at least this form of presentation enables comparisons to be made at a glance.

If the method has a shortcoming, it is that it may cater well for *proportions*, but is less satisfactory as a way of expressing *quantities*. You will notice that, in the case of the first diagram, the total expressed is £48m; but for 1935 it is £4516m, a total nearly a hundred times greater in money terms. Yet the size of all the circles is exactly the same. You will see more about this in Unit 3.

Nevertheless, whether alone and unaided, or whether in conjunction with some other visual medium such as a map, pie charts can be extremely informative, as in Figure 3.12. Here the map shows the rate levied annually by the local authorities on the relief of poverty at the time of the Poor Law Amendment Act in 1834. The amounts are expressed in terms of the old currency. The lighter areas on the map may mean that these were areas of less poverty, so that less spending was required. Alternatively, it may mean that these were areas where the local authorities were either unable, or unwilling, to pay out large sums to the poor. Since some of the light-coloured areas include some of the areas where there were large pockets of poverty, both in urban and rural areas, it seems likely that the second explanation is to be preferred.

The pie charts on the right of the Figure convey further information on the same subject. You ought to observe that the *dates* of the three separate rows of diagrams are different, and the *sources of information* are not the same, though two of them relate to the same English city, York. In which one of the pie charts does the total of the segments come to 100? How do

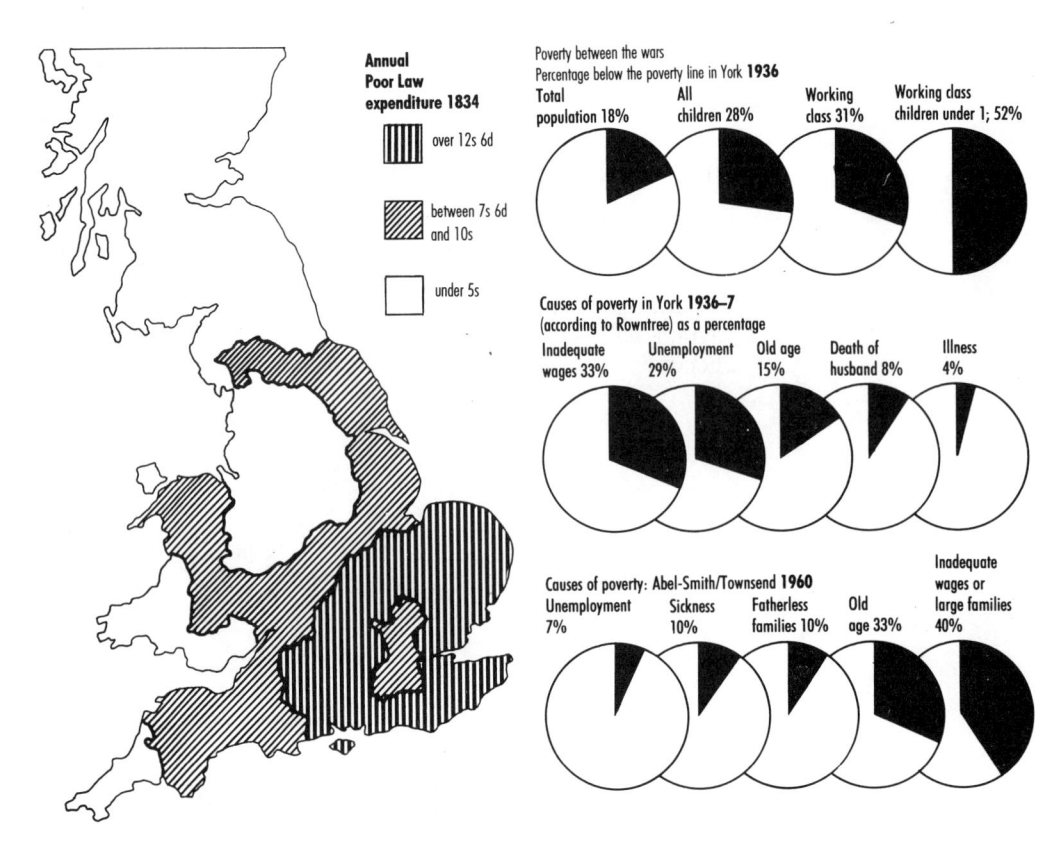

Fig 3.12
Combining maps and pie charts

you explain that one of the other totals is *less than* 100, and the other *more than* 100? Try to work out before you read the next paragraph.

The segments in the third row (1960) add exactly to 100. This is because the five categories dealt with are defined so as to include *all* the causes of poverty; there are not any other causes left over. That perhaps gives a clue to the second row, which, when totalled comes only to 89. This must mean that, according to Rowntree's survey in York, 11% of the poverty investigated did not come about through the five causes dealt with in the charts, but from some other causes. The first row, with a total of 129, on the face of it seems even more baffling, until you look closely at the four categories dealt with: then you will see that they are such as to be *incapable of being added together*. The second, third and fourth categories overlap, and the first pie chart is something quite different from the others.

BAR CHARTS

These are bars or blocks of different dimensions, laid alongside each other to give information visually on the subject they are dealing with. The bars may either be *vertical* or *horizontal*. They are usually bars in two dimensions, but sometimes they are blocks in three dimensions.

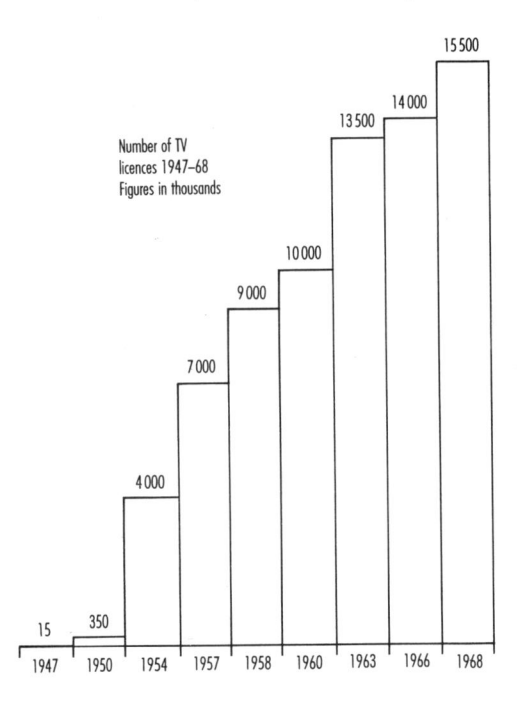

Fig 3.13
Bar charts: TV licence sales;
1947–1968

CHAPTER THREE THE USE OF STATISTICAL MATERIAL

Figure 3.13 illustrates the growth of the number of television licences (expressed in thousands, or 000) issued between 1947 and 1968. Can you read it? It tells us that the number rose from a mere 15 000 in 1947 to 15½m in 1968, a thousand-fold increase. There are a few things to note. The first is that the intervals between the measurements is not exactly the same: one-, two-, three- and four-year intervals may be picked out from the dates at the foot of the diagram. This means that if we try to translate this diagram into a graph, we shall have a number of years for which we have to *extrapolate* the figures. The second thing is that the increase in the number of licences does not grow at a uniform rate, but in spurts. Where, numerically, does it increase the *most slowly*, and where the *most rapidly*?

The second bar chart (Fig 3.14) illustrates different kinds of agriculture in Great Britain between 1867 and 1939. To help you to read it the figures, in thousand acres, are placed alongside each bar in the graph. Can you read it?

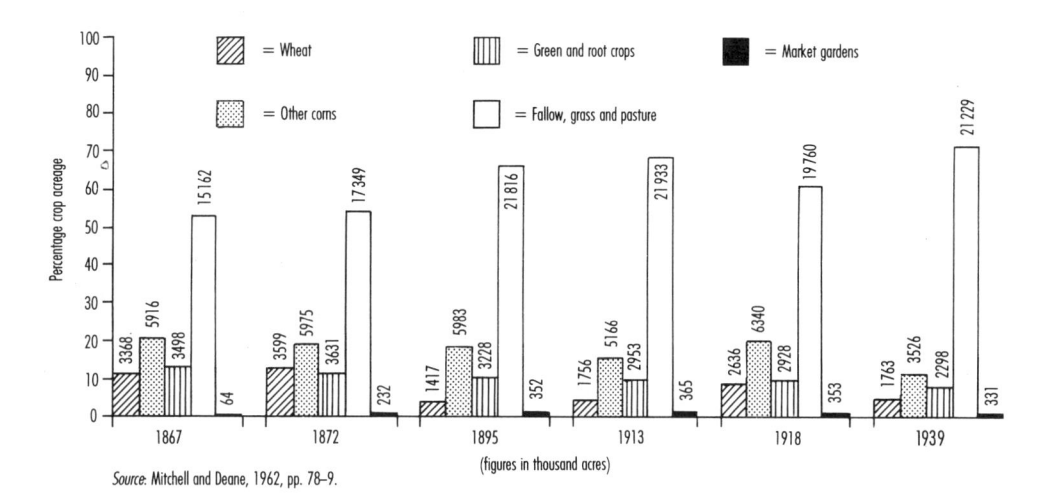

Fig 3.14
Bar charts: crop acreage in Great Britain

Source: Mitchell and Deane, 1962, pp. 78–9.

Again, there are a few things to note. The first is that the selection of years seems to be quite arbitrary; possibly these are the years for which the information is available, or which seem to the compiler of the table to be for some reason the most important years to choose. The second is that – overall – the total acreage under crop does not seem to change very much: the largest acreage seems to be in 1895, when it was 32 796 000, and the smallest in 1867, when it was 28 008 000.

The diagram also illustrates one of the weaknesses of bar charts. There is a great difference between the grass and pasture acreage for 1913 (21 933 000) and the market garden acreage for 1867 (64 000). It is almost impossible to represent this clearly on the bar chart. To show the latter in such a way as to be visible and accurate, it would be necessary to have a scale which, for the other figure, would run off the page. Bar charts are obviously much more effective when the quantities they illustrate are more nearly equal than in this case.

STATISTICAL PICTURES

There are too many of these to deal with at any length. Their number and variety depend largely on their author. Some of these pictures are easy to interpret, but others are much more difficult. Let us take three.

The first picture (Fig 3.15) has something in common with a pie chart. It shows government expenditure as a proportion of Gross National Product in certain years between 1890 and 1970. Its strength is that it illustrates the *proportionate* growth of government spending very effectively; its weakness is that the 'pies' employed are all the same size, and conceal the fact that the GNP rose in these years from little more than £1 500m to well over £45 000m.

The second picture (Fig 3.16) has something in common with a bar chart, and illustrates the growth in police strength in England and Wales from 1856 to 1970. Its meaning is clarified by the actual figures given on the left, alongside the dates. It has, however, a major fault: the left-hand axis *slopes*, and this slope makes it hard to see by how much any one of the bars differs from another. The use of small cartoon policemen is a nice idea dramatically, each one of them representing 3 000 policemen. But the way they are arranged, in closely packed ranks, with each policeman halfway between the two behind him, makes it much harder for the eye to estimate the quantities.

The third picture (Fig 3.17) has something in common with a graph (to which we turn in the next section). It deals with the relative changes in the uses of primary fuels such as natural

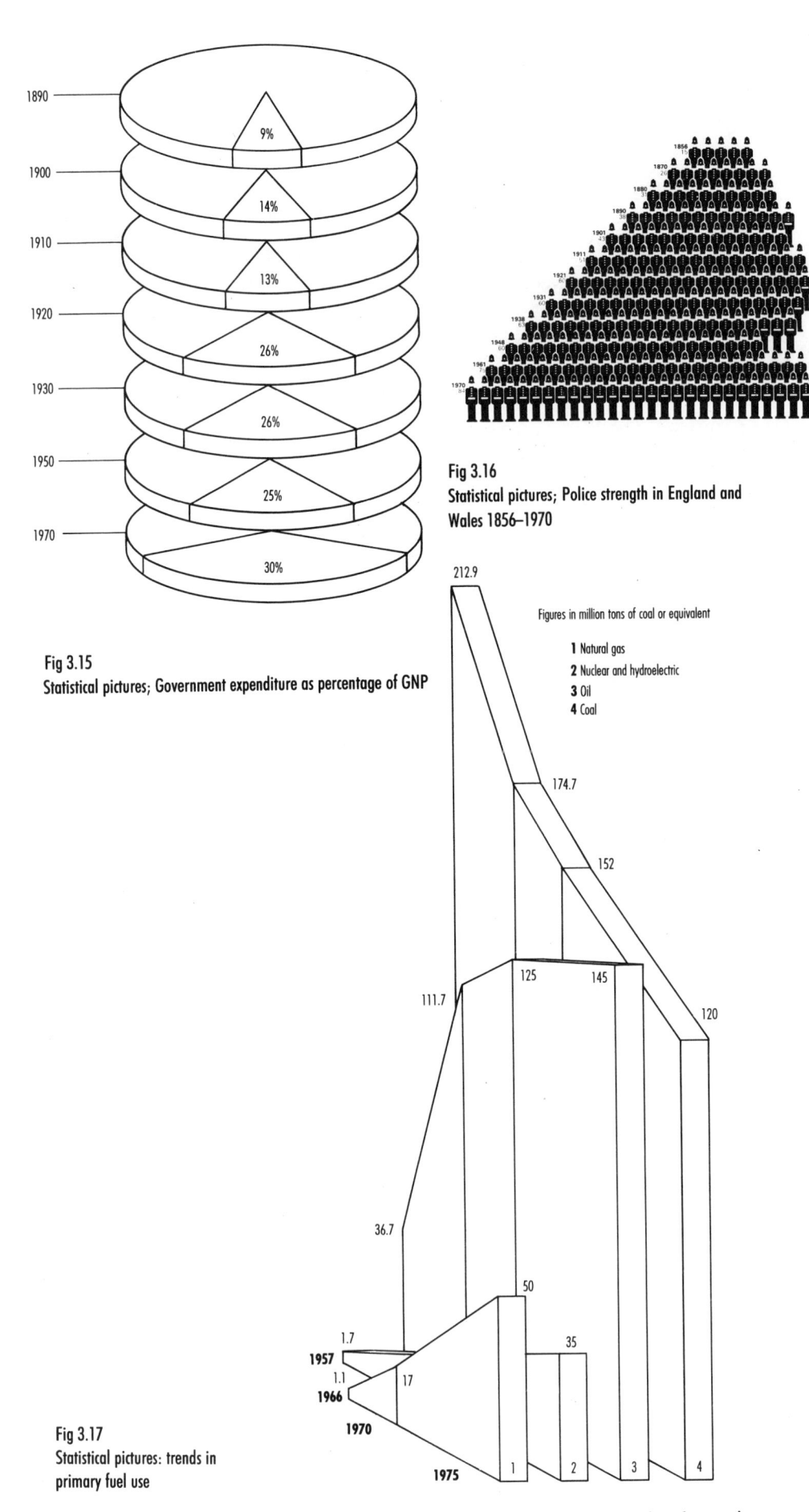

46 CHAPTER THREE USING STATISTICS AND EVIDENCE MATERIAL

Fig 3.15
Statistical pictures; Government expenditure as percentage of GNP

Fig 3.16
Statistical pictures; Police strength in England and Wales 1856–1970

Fig 3.17
Statistical pictures: trends in primary fuel use

Figures in million tons of coal or equivalent
1 Natural gas
2 Nuclear and hydroelectric
3 Oil
4 Coal

gas, nuclear and hydroelectric power, oil and coal. Its strength is the dramatic contrast it shows between trends in the uses of coal and the other fuels. One of its difficulties is that, since the diagram is three-dimensional, it is not immediately easy to quantify the amounts shown for 1966 and 1970. A number of books, however, use picture diagrams, and students must learn how to read and understand these, and possibly try to use them themselves.

(3) Graphs

2.3 Graphs

Graphs are a well-established method of representing, accurately and legibly, information which would take much longer to put into words. Outside Mathematics, the use of graphs is usual in Geography, Economics and most of the physical sciences. They may already be familiar to you for your other work.

Graphs are usually drawn on squared paper (*graph paper*) against two axes, a vertical axis and a horizontal axis. One axis represents one of the variables involved in the presentation, and the other axis represents the other variable. You locate a point with your pencil at which one of the values given coincides with the other, and you repeat this location process for all the values you are given in the data. Then you connect up the points you have made, and produce a *profile* which expresses in a diagrammatic form the relationships between one set of values and the other. In this way, you are able to express graphically a sales curve using information such as the following:

Items purchased	Prices
150	£1
100	£2
50	£3
30	£4
20	£5

The intermediate position for prices not given in the data can be determined by quantifying the points along the connecting line. The steepness, or shallowness, of the slope illustrates the *rate of change* between intermediate positions.

CONVEYING INFORMATION

In Social and Economic History, graphs are frequently used as a convenient way of conveying information. A graph may easily be produced from a table (as above); conversely, it is possible to translate information from a graph into the form of a table. Graphs have their proper role not only on examination papers, but in coursework too.

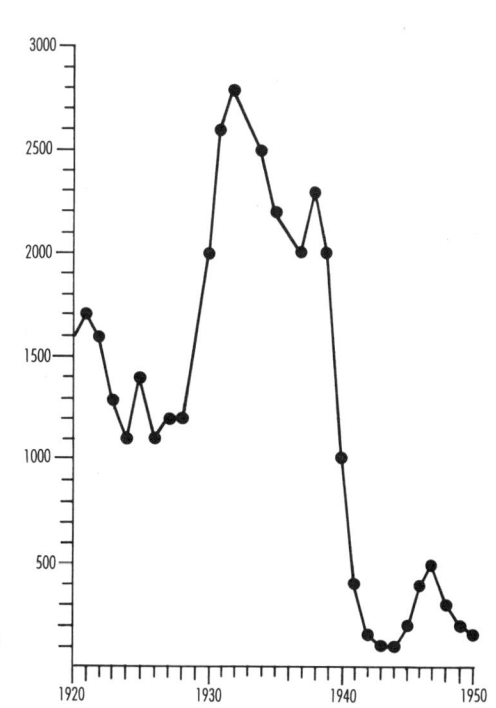

Fig 3.18
Graphs: total numbers registered as unemployed (000s)

Let us take three such graphs. The first (Fig 3.18) relates to the number of persons registered as unemployed in Britain between 1920 and 1950. The numbers can thus be seen year by year during this period of thirty years, against a vertical axis which goes up in thousands to 3m. For 1932, for instance, you can see that the figure is 2 800 000, and for 1943 it is 100 000. Can you work out how many people were registered as unemployed in 1925 for yourself? The *steepness* of the slope shows rapid changes between 1928 and 1932, and between 1939 and 1943. It ought to be possible to use your other knowledge to mark in the period of the World Depression, and the years of the Second World War, and to understand the reasons why unemployment should have been high in the one case, and low in the other.

The second graph (Fig 3.19) has *two* profiles. The upper one illustrates the total spent on imported goods, such as raw materials and foodstuffs. The lower one shows the amount of money raised by British exports of manufactures and other goods. Again, the horizontal axis measures years, and this time the vertical axis measures millions of pounds (briefly, £m). The shaded space between the two is the amount by which the first figure exceeded the second, i.e. the 'trade gap'.

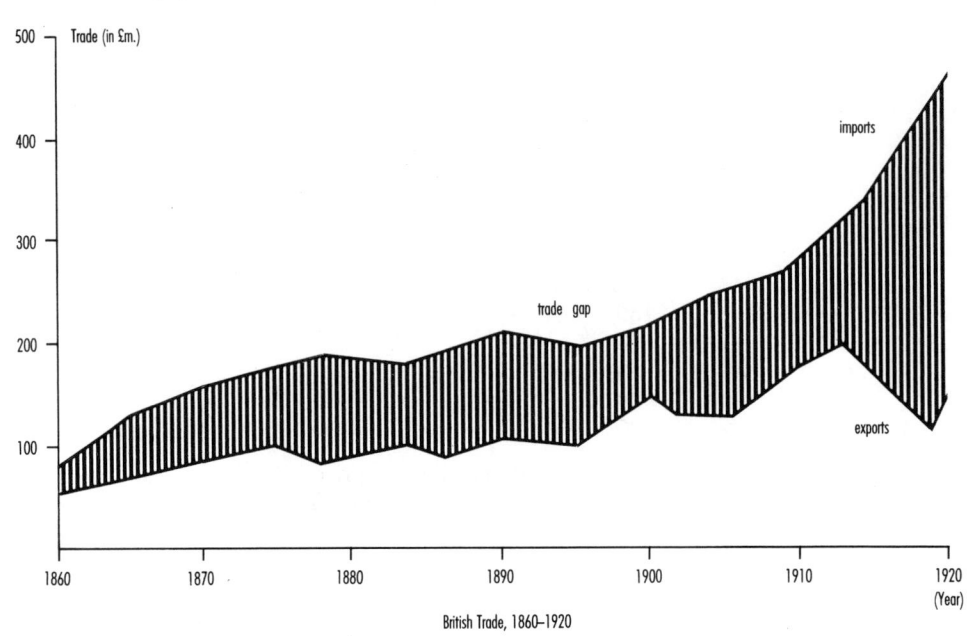

Fig 3.19
Graphs: British trade; 1860–1920

British Trade, 1860–1920

The graph shows that at the beginning of the period Britain exported about £50m-worth of goods per year, and imported about £75m-worth. It shows that British exports increased quite slowly, with perceptible falls in the late 1870s, the mid–1880s and at the time of the Boer War, 1900–1902. It also shows that British exports fell off sharply at the time of the First World War. British imports, on the other hand, increased fairly consistently, beginning to climb quite sharply after 1909, and increasing further after 1914.

One thing to note is that these are cash figures in £s, and do not take any account of changes in the value of money. A fall in the value of money, i.e. a degree of inflation, will mean that an apparent rise in exports will be offset by a price rise. On the other hand, an increase in the value of money, i.e. a degree of deflation, might mean that although the bill for imports has gone down, in real terms the country may have been receiving as much in the way of goods as before. There is more about *money prices* and *real prices* in the next Unit.

The other thing to notice is that a graph like this is about visible trade in real commodities (whether imports or exports) of the sort that can be loaded on to a boat for shipment. Of course, physical goods are not the only sort that Britain exports. We provide banking facilities for which foreigners are required to pay. We provide other business services, such as shipping and insurance. We lend money to foreign governments on which they pay us interest. These services mean that the deficit on the visible account is more than offset by these other sources of income. There is more about *visible* and *invisible* trade in the next Unit.

The third graph (Fig 3.20) deals with percentages, and illustrates the different growth-rates of Britain and the members of the European Economic Community in the period 1958–66. Once again, the years go across the bottom of the graph, but this time on the vertical axis we have what is called an *index*. This is based on what is called a *base year* – in this case 1958, which is called 100. After the base year, any increase will be shown in a figure *larger* than 100, by adding on the percentage growth. Any fall will be shown by a figure *smaller* than 100, after the percentage diminution has been knocked off. More about *indices* is to be found in the next Unit of this chapter.

The fact that the two lines in the graph both begin at the origin does not mean that EEC countries and Britain had *no economy at all* in 1958; in fact the two lines in the graph both begin at 100. It should be noted that the *origin* is not the same thing as 0, the *quantity*. Nor does it mean that the two were *equal* in 1958. In fact the EEC was much bigger. It means that whatever the sizes of the two economies, the profile shows in what proportion they grew.

Statistical material of all kinds is useful in coursework, and should be used to illustrate whatever assignments it is available to help. It can be translated from one form to another in order to be more suitable for the particular use you have in mind. Statistical evidence may also form the basis of coursework exercises or examination questions to test your knowledge and your skills in the subject.

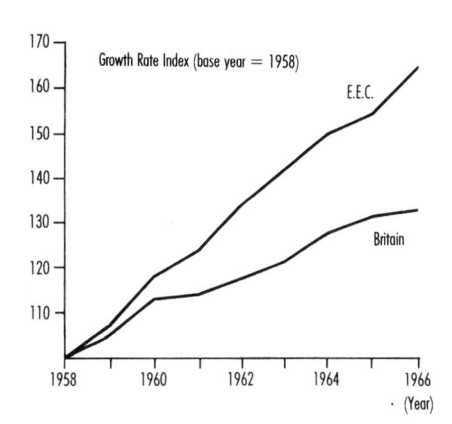

Fig 3.20
Graphs: Economic growth rate of
Britain compared with the EEC

UNIT 3 COMMON PROBLEMS WITH STATISTICS

" Look out for traps "

The purpose of this part of the chapter is to point out to students common problems and misunderstandings in the use of statistics.

3.1 Misleading averages

There is more than one way to carry out an exercise which is very common in Arithmetic, yet the results are by no means the same. Let us take an imaginary example relating to a number of men earning money by working in a factory. Suppose that the total annual wage-bill looks like this:

Managing Director	1	£250 000	£250 000
Works Manager	1	£90 000	£90 000
Department Managers	6	£50 000	£300 000
Under-Managers	6	£15 000	£90 000
Foreman	10	£13 000	£130 000
Deputy Foreman	2	£12 500	£25 000
Operatives	22	£5 000	£110 000
Apprentices	2	£2 500	£5 000
	50		1 000 000

MEANS

An arithmetical *mean* is perhaps the commonest form of average. It is calculated in this example by totalling the wage bill and dividing this total by the number of earners. The average annual wage is therefore £1 000 000 ÷ 50, or £20 000 per person. In fact, no one earns exactly that figure, the nearest to it being Under-Managers who earn £15 000 each. But perhaps this average gives rather an optimistic picture. To say that average earnings are £20 000 a year sounds quite good to the outsider – but in fact, if you look at the table, you will see that 42 people out of a total of 50 in fact earn *less* than this figure. If you were designing something for trade union consumption, therefore, this might well be the sort of presentation you would choose to employ.

MEDIANS

A smaller figure is provided by *median* earnings. The two Deputy Foremen with £12 500 each may be said to earn the median earnings because they are in the middle of the whole group, i.e. there are 24 people who earn less than they do, and 24 people who earn more. This figure is at least earned by someone on the table, and it gives a rather more modest impression of earnings than the earlier one.

MODES

The *mode* is the number which is most frequently met with in the table. By this reckoning, the modal earning is £5000 a year, since there are far more people earning this figure than any other. If you stopped any one of the work-force as he came out through the factory gate, and

Averages

asked him what he earned, this is the answer you would be most likely to get. You will note, too, that this gives the most modest impression of all – exactly a quarter of the mean figure.

Averages can therefore vary quite considerably, and you have to be sure which sort you are using. If an unscrupulous statistician constructed the table he might give you quite a misleading impression by choosing the form of average that best suited his own purposes. Of course, if you are talking about the heights of a large number of men (say a thousand), when they vary by small amounts between fairly close limits (say from 5ft to 6ft 6in), the mean is the best and fairest way of calculating the average. But if you are talking about earnings, where a large number of people earn less than the mean, and a very small number of people earn enormous sums far above it, the mean is perhaps less useful.

3.2 Misleading bar charts

Some dangers in bar charts

The information conveyed by a bar chart depends very much on the way that it is presented. Let us suppose that you are a manufacturer of candy-bars, and are advertising your latest addition to the market, the 'Elephant Crunch', as against the 'Crocodile Crackle' or the 'Tiger Bite'. Your monthly sales figures may be something like this:

January	2 950 000
February	3 100 000
March	3 150 000
April	3 250 000
May	3 500 000

The figures for the candy-bar of your choice may be little different from the other two, but this is the one you have decided to advertise and you have to be careful how you present your data. One way would be as in Figure 3.21. This may seem to you to be quite impressive, until your advertising manager points out that a lot of space is being wasted at the *bottom* of the chart, and you could express the information much more effectively by altering the presentation.

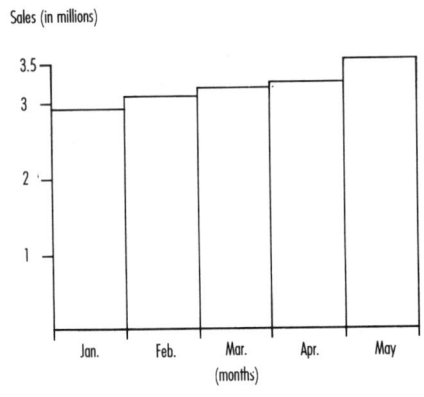

Fig 3.21
Misleading bar charts: Candy-bar sales

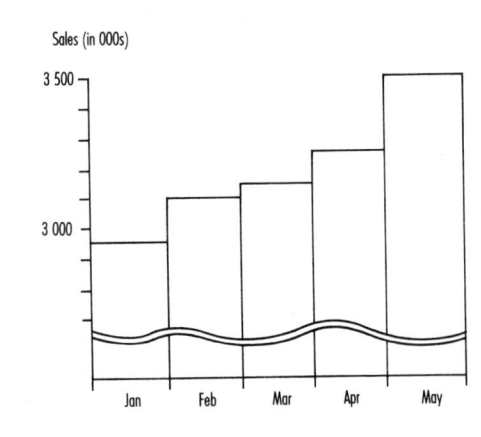

Fig 3.22
Misleading bar charts: Candy-bar sales (interrupted columns)

You can do this by 'interrupting' the columns, as in Figure 3.22, so that only the *upper* parts are illustrated. This makes the differences between the respective heights of the columns much more obvious, though the information conveyed is just the same as it was before. The trouble arises when you forget that the columns are interrupted, and make some such observation as 'The table shows that between January and May sales more than doubled' – in fact they increased by less than 20%. See also *Misleading picture-diagrams*.

3.3 Misleading graphs

Watch out for graphs

What has been said above about bar charts is also true of graphs. These can be drawn to suggest exactly opposite conclusions. One type of graph can suggest inferences which are modest, but accurate. The other sort, by concentrating on a detailed display of the information, can produce an illustration which is much more dramatic. Let us, for example, take this table showing the increase in the government's public spending in recent years:

CHAPTER THREE   **COMMON PROBLEMS WITH STATISTICS**   51

1969 £16 500m
1974 £16 600m
1979 £17 000m
1984 £18 000m
1989 £21 000m

❝ Whoopee graphs ❞

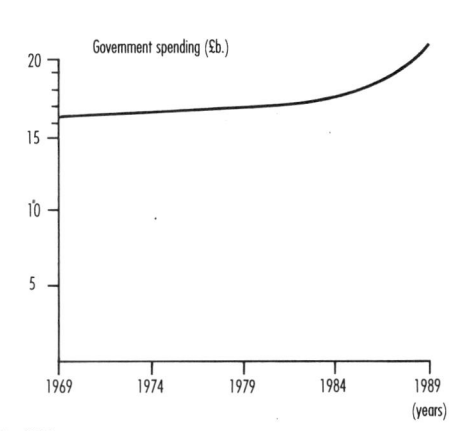

Fig 3.23
Misleading graphs: Government spending (£b)

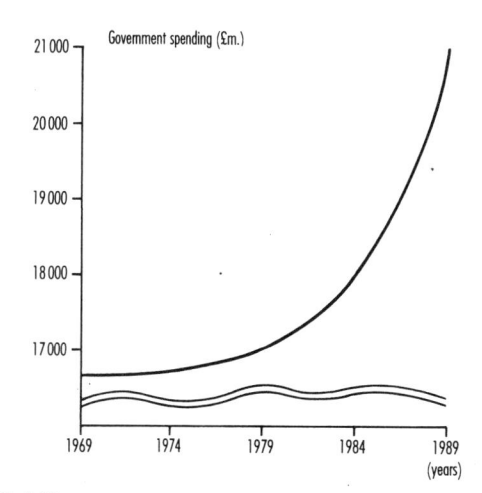

Fig 3.24
Misleading graphs: Government spending (£m)
(interrupted version)

Compare the two graphs (Figs 3.23 and 3.24). The first (Fig 3.23) shows, on its vertical axis, government spending from zero upwards, and is calibrated in billions. Figure 3.24 carries the same information, but it is abbreviated at the foot by a similar interruption to the one in the bar chart (Fig 3.22), and portrays what is evidently a much more startling growth of spending. This latter type of graph is sometimes referred to as a 'Whoopee' graph.

The first graph shows a marked, though not excessive, growth of public spending, and truly represents it as a growth of about 27%. The second is misleading, and represents the increase as more than a quintupling of spending. If the graphs were produced in the House of Commons, it would all depend whether the minister in question was trying to show how *prudent* the government was in holding down these increases in spending, or how *generous* the government was in comparison with its niggardly opponents.

3.4 Misleading picture diagrams

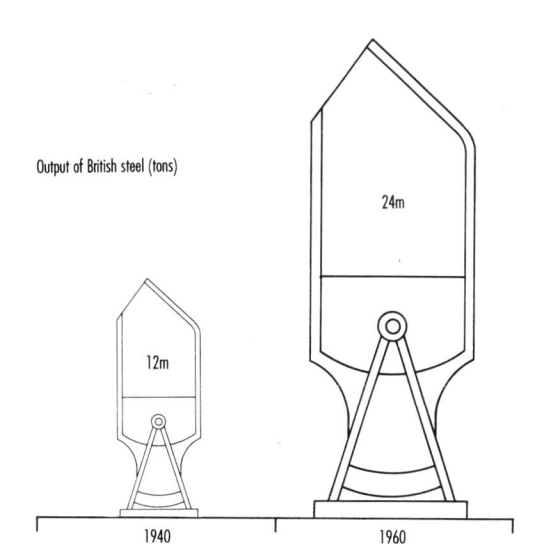

❝ Pictures can lie ❞

Fig 3.25
Misleading picture-diagrams:
output of British steel (tons)

Something has already been said about exaggeration brought about by the width of columns in bar charts. This is also true of picture diagrams. Let us take the following example, taken from statistics showing that between 1940 and 1960 the output of British steel doubled, i.e. from 12m tons to 24m tons per year. This information can be expressed as in Figure 3.25.

The symbol used in the picture-diagram is a Bessemer converter. The one for the steel output of 1960 is twice as high as the one for 1940, and that is the message the picture is meant to convey. But in fact, the converter is also twice as wide, so that it represents a four-fold rather than a two-fold increase, and this could be very misleading to the unwary. But this is not the worst. In fact, Bessemer converters have *depth* as well as height and width, since they are three-dimensional objects. The increase suggested by the picture is thus an eight-fold increase, instead of the mere doubling that the statistics actually tell us.

This exaggeration is bound to happen whenever any three-dimensional object is drawn in a diagram-picture, whether it is bags of gold to represent revenue, or little battleships to represent the Royal Navy. To avoid the error it is generally better to steer clear of picture-diagrams, and to stick to bar charts and graphs.

3.5 Incomplete evidence

"Evidence with gaps"

From time to time you will discover that the evidence you can find is *incomplete*. The use in tables of a dash ('–') and zero ('0') has already been mentioned. The dash signifies that the figure is small, or unimportant, or even unknown. The zero means a zero quantity, nil or nought. The same thing sometimes applies in the case of graphs. For instance, there may be a gap in a set of statistics relating to immigration in a given year, although the years on either side are well-known; or there may be a gap in population statistics, for instance for 1941, when there was the Second World War and no census took place. In some cases you may find a break in the graph profile; in others, a dotted line connecting the last two firm pieces of information, or even a dotted line projected into the future, to cover a reasonable prediction of a future figure that has not yet occurred.

EXTRAPOLATION

In many cases it would be reasonable to make an estimate for the missing figures. If we know that the price of a loaf of bread in 1945 was 4½d, and in 1960 was 1s 3d, it would be fairly safe to assume that in 1953 the price was somewhere between the two. The process of making an intelligent guess for figures which are lacking is known as the process of *extrapolation*. In the same way, if a quantity is missing on a graph, it might be sensible to put in the dotted line referred to above.

All the same, we have to admit that what we are putting in is no more than a *guess*. There may be a freak in the prices of bread, which means that in 1953 the figure was outside the limits suggested by the prices given for 1945 and 1960. Likewise, when we put in our dotted line on the graph, we may be suggesting a rise, when in fact there was a fall. This is because we cannot be sure what the missing quantities are.

In the same way, the use of quinquennial averages (or some other sort of averages) on a graph conceals the many ups-and-downs of individual years. In Figure 3.10, for instance, the figures for 1930–34 may conceal variations. Though the quinquennial average is 6 733 thousand tons, it may well be that more detailed figures would give sharper evidence of the start in Britain of the World Depression. The individual figures for these five years (in 000 tons) may well be 9 000, 7 500, 3 050, 5 515 and 8 600; that gives a total of 33 665, and a quinquennial average of 6 733. Indeed, such an average is intended to smooth out the variations. If you were to put the variations on a graph you would finish with a profile like the cutting teeth of a saw.

Extrapolation, in any case, is not always feasible. No one would argue, for example, that because a 2p coin, and a 10p coin, and a £ coin are all circular, that we can safely assume that a 20p coin and a 50p coin are also circular. We should only extrapolate when it is reasonable to do so.

3.6 English, British and UK statistics

Mistakes are often made because students fail to notice that the basis of comparison has been changed. If you look again at Figure 3.11 you will see that this is the case here. No close comparison between the pie charts is possible if they have different geographical bases. In Figure 3.11, the figures are successively for England and Wales, for Great Britain, and for the United Kingdom. It is important to be clear about the differences.

ENGLAND AND WALES

"England, Britain and the United Kingdom"

Many statistics are supplied on this basis. Figures for England and Wales, if more detailed, are sometimes given separately, but they are more usually presented together. Such figures, of course, exclude those for Scotland.

GREAT BRITAIN

This is the largest island of the group, containing England, Wales and Scotland, and all the adjacent smaller islands. The name is sometimes shortened to 'Britain'.

THE BRITISH ISLES

This comprises all the islands of the group, including Ireland. It is chiefly a geographical term, and is less used in Social and Economic History.

UNITED KINGDOM

This came into common use during the present century. After 1800, it meant the same as the British Isles, for at that time, under the Act of Union, Ireland was linked with Great Britain. After 1922, however, when autonomy was granted to the southern part of Ireland, the term changed to its present meaning – the *United Kingdom of Great Britain and Northern Ireland*.

You should always take care to verify, when you study statistics, to which of these groups your figures relate. Likewise, when you produce a table of your own, you should be sure to make clear which of these groups you are talking about when you tabulate your information. On no account should you allow yourself to slip from one to another without noticing.

3.7 Money prices and real prices

> **The problem of money prices and real prices**

All prices take the form of a *ratio* between money available and goods available. If we are trading in oranges at the market, a surplus of oranges will mean that in money terms the price of oranges will go down. Conversely, a shortage of oranges will mean that the price of oranges will go up. The same applies to the supply of money. An increase in the supply of money will mean that the price of oranges goes up; a reduction in the supply of money will mean that a smaller amount of money will secure a larger number of oranges, i.e. that the price of oranges will go down.

When the supply of money increases, of course, it is not just the price of oranges that is affected – *all* prices will tend to rise. Likewise, a fall in the supply of money will bring a general fall in prices. At one time, this was known as the *quantity theory of money*.

INFLATION

The situation in which more and more money is created, but the supply of goods remains about the same, so that more money is required to make purchases, is usually known as *inflation*. In modern times it is not uncommon. Nor, unless it gets out of hand, does it do much damage. This is because it has the twin effects of lowering the level of indebtedness and of stimulating trade and manufacture. It is only when it develops into *galloping inflation*, with prices rising day-by-day and hour-by-hour that it does lasting damage to the economy.

DEFLATION

The opposite situation is less common, though there have been a number of occasions in history when it has happened. If, for some reason, the supply of money falls, or fails to expand, e.g. if it is based on gold, and the supply of gold becomes restricted, whilst at the same time the supply of goods increases, e.g. because of technological advances, then it is likely that prices will fall. This is known as *deflation*. It has some obvious attractions for people, in that the same amount of income will buy more and more goods. But there are serious side-effects. Because each repayment buys more, it increases the burden of debt. Also, because it restricts profit levels, it discourages trade and manufacture and may lead to unemployment.

Changes in the value of money naturally affect the meaning of a statistical table. Take another look, for example, at Figure 3.19. We see that the common money value of British exports in 1860 was £50m, and the money value of imports was £75m. In 1914 exports were worth nearly £250m and imports over £400m. Does this mean that British exports increased five-fold in volume and imports more than five-fold in the course of the nineteenth century? If the value of money had been constant, it would. However, sometimes, and for most of the century, it fell slightly by reason of inflation, and towards the end of the century there was a time when it rose slightly by reason of deflation. Overall, it *fell*, i.e. prices rose. Thus, in terms of volume, trade increased four-fold rather than five; the rest of the apparent increase is not a real one, but due to inflation.

Eliminating changes in money value

It is often useful to eliminate changes in the value of money from our calculations, and we can do this in one of two ways:

1. We give the *volume figure* for trade, instead of the *sterling amounts* they are worth. Hence we speak of yards of cotton cloth, numbers of iron girders, tons of coal and so on. Then we can see accurately whether trade is increasing or not.

2. We discount changes in prices by giving the value of the goods as if they were measured in terms of a single one of the years in the table. This is specially useful if the goods are not the sort that can be physically measured, but are, for example, services such as freight charges in shipping.

The distinction between *real prices* and *money prices* are specially important when we are talking about wages and earnings. If, for example, a man's wages double, but prices double at the same time, then he is no better off. Nor, if his wages are halved, is he any worse off if prices are halved at the same time. But the two things do not often coincide. We discover, for example, that in the 1890s the wages of working men were stationary, but that consumer prices were falling slowly, so that they were better off. Earlier, in the later stages of the Napoleonic Wars (1800–1814) we discover that though prices were rising sharply, many workers were earning very little more, so that they were worse off. When we are looking at earnings, therefore, it is desirable to distinguish clearly between *real wages* and *money wages*.

Another way of achieving the same objective, i.e. eliminating fluctuations in the value of money, is by employing *indices*. These have the same effect as example 2 immediately above. More detailed consideration is given to this subject later in this Unit.

3.8 Old and new currencies

❝ New money for old money ❞

Until 1971, the pound sterling was subdivided into shillings and pence. There were 20 shillings to the pound, and each shilling was divided into 12 pence, so that there were 240 pence to the pound. There were paper notes for the £1 and for ten shillings, and coins for smaller denominations – for a half-penny, a penny, three pence, six pence, a shilling, two shillings and half-a-crown (or two shillings and sixpence). Farthings (quarter-pennies) had already been phased out, and threepenny pieces were soon to follow.

DECIMALISATION

Though this rather cumbersome currency was backed by tradition and a good deal of sentiment, the government decided on the eve of joining the European Community to *decimalize* its currency in order to bring it into line with the French franc and the German mark. The pound sterling was retained as the basic unit, but it was now divided into 100 'new' pence, conveniently abbreviated as 'p' instead of 'd'. In fact the 'new' penny was much smaller than the jumbo-sized old penny, though it was worth more than twice as much. The shilling was transformed into 5p, and two shillings into 10p – actually the same coins remained in circulation. Sixpence (2½p) and half-a-crown (12½p) were phased out, and a 'new' twopenny piece came into use. Paper notes for 50p (ten shillings) and £1 disappeared and were replaced by coins. A coin also came into use for 20p (four shillings).

In many books, and all those published before 1971, the old denominations were used, and this may be confusing to the modern reader unfamiliar with the traditional currency:

1 'new' penny (p)	2.4 old pennies (d)
2p	4.8d
5p	12 pence or 1 shilling (s)
10p	2s
20p	4s
50p	10s

One of the tiresome exercises set for generations of schoolchildren by their teachers had been to calculate sums of money (say 3s 6d) as percentages of a pound (17½%). Your more elderly relatives may even be able to tell you how this was done. Now, however, percentages and pennies became the same thing – 1p was 1% of a pound, 5p was 5% and so on. At least this meant the removal of one source of confusion!

CHAPTER THREE **COMMON PROBLEMS WITH STATISTICS**

3.9 Indices

❝What is an index?❞

Section 3.7 of this Unit referred to the use of *indices*. An *index* is a convenient statistical way of eliminating changes, e.g. changes in the value of money, which would distort figures as given in a table if the variations were not taken into account. The practical advantage of such a procedure is that indices enable a graph or a table to be constructed which eliminates unwanted variables.

An index is a figure calculated as a percentage of a given year, referred to as the *base year*, i.e. the year against which the comparison is made. If output of, say, locomotives in the base year – say 1948 – is 3480, the output of succeeding years is calculated as a percentage of this figure. If the output of locomotives in the following year is 4176, we say that the index of locomotive production is 120, because it has gone up by 696, i.e. by 20%. If by 1958 the output is only 1740, we say that the index is 50, because it has fallen by half.

If you refer back to Figure 3.20, you will see that the indices for the industrial growth of the United Kingdom and the countries of the European Community are being compared. Whatever the industrial situation of the two groups may be in 1958 – and it certainly would not be one of parity – the figure that is given for that year is 100. This does not mean that at that point the two groups are *equal*; but simply that it is from that year that the comparison is being made. By 1959, the economy of the UK has grown by 4%, i.e. it now stands at 104, whilst the economies of the EEC countries stand at 107, i.e. they have grown by 7%. If you look at the table, you will see that the same thing happens in subsequent years, until, by 1966, the two indices stand respectively at 130 and 165. That is to say that between 1958 and 1966 the British economy grew by 30%, but that the economies of the EEC grew by 65%. This information eliminates all the variables which might obscure the picture. What the table shows, in a dramatic form, is the gap which steadily opens up between the EEC countries and the UK in terms of industrial growth, with the UK steadily falling behind the other continental countries.

COST OF LIVING INDEX

❝...for example, the Cost of Living index❞

Indices are encountered in many forms of statistics to do with trading figures, living standards etc. They are perhaps most familiar in the form of the *cost of living index*. This enables people to see readily how living standards at any one time compare with some earlier time. It is of course important to see how such an index is calculated.

In order to see how the present cost of living can be compared with that in an earlier year, a formula has to be devised from which to create a reasonable index. Assuming that the most important items of spending in a worker's budget are food, clothing, travelling and rent, we can invent a basis on which to measure. Suppose we allow a 50% weighting for food, a 15% weighting for clothes, 10% for travel and 25% for rent. We can then base our new cost-of-living figure on the relative amount by which the four variables have changed over a period. If rent has doubled, but the other items have remained the same, the effect on the index will be less than if it had been food that had increased in price. This is because food has twice the weighting of rent.

This, of course, is purely an imaginary example; the real cost-of-living index has far more than four items in it, and makes allowances for most of the things that wages have to be spent on. But the final figure is valuable in calculating how the cost of living changes over time.

❝A few crooked dodges❞

Two reservations should be made about the use of this, or any other, index:

1. You should note carefully which is the *base year*. The more recent it is, the less revealing will it be. For instance, the cost of living will not have changed as much since 1988 as, for example, since 1980. Also, both figures will have changed less than an index based on 1960. In fact, one well-established way of concealing changes is to shift the base year forward, in order to be able to point out how little things have altered. Nevertheless, the base year can also be pushed too far back. There would be little use in comparing the cost of living over a very long period of time, say since 1450 or 1688, unless we are prepared to admit that the way the index has been made up has changed. Mortgage interest payments, for instance, are much more important in 1989 than they were in 1689, but the blacksmith's charges for shoeing your horse are much less important now than they were then. A long-term index would therefore have to be much simpler if it was to be of value.
2. You should observe (if you can) whether the formula for calculating the index has been changed. Some changes, of course, have to be made over a period of time – for instance when licences have to be taken out for colour TVs. To ignore such changes would distort the index. But equally it would be wrong to manipulate the items in the index for other reasons, e.g. to leave out items whose price has increased simply in order to be able to show that the index has not changed very much. Governments, many of whose

out-payments are linked to the cost-of-living index, have a very powerful motive for manipulating the index. Students have a more disinterested view, and should be aware of the potential dishonesty.

Indices are important for far more things than calculating the cost of living. They can be used for studying economic growth, as in Figure 3.20, or for many other things to do with manufacture and trade. Some of these are studied below.

3.10 Visible and invisible trade

❝ Visibles and Invisibles ❞

VISIBLE TRADE

The physical items in which a country deals for its trade are known as *visibles*. Britain, for example, over a long period, has imported raw materials (cotton, iron ore, oil, rubber etc.) and foodstuffs (beef, wheat, cocoa etc.), but exported manufactured articles (shirts, locomotives, motor-cars, dynamos etc.). It is therefore possible to compare imports with exports on a purely physical basis, either by volume or by value. The former has the advantage of eliminating price-changes.

INVISIBLE TRADE

There are other items, however, which go towards making up a country's *invisible trade*. Lloyd's of London, for example, provide insurance services for shipping, and many foreigners may choose to insure their ships in this country – a service for which they have to pay. Britain may therefore buy wheat from abroad (which is visible), and pay for it in insurance services (which are invisible). There are many other services to do with banking, brokerage and finance which add to Britain's invisible exports. The cost of such items frequently enables the country to import more goods than it exports, and still pay for them.

Many *invisibles* work both ways. Tourism is a case in point. When British tourists travel abroad they count (oddly enough) as an *import*. This is because when touring they provide foreigners with a claim to our resources when they spend sterling, just as if they were importing commodities. Likewise, foreigners spending their money in this country when they are touring count as an *export* because they provide Britain with a claim to other people's resources, just as they would if Britain was exporting commodities. Thus, if foreign tourists in Britain spend more than British tourists travelling abroad, we shall be better off. If the reverse is the case, we shall be making a loss in that department.

Although it really makes no difference whether we are dealing with visibles or invisibles in making our calculations, students should notice that the two categories are often listed separately, as though invisibles were somehow special. Certainly, when you are working out the country's overall trade position, you have to take both of them into account.

BALANCE OF TRADE

❝ The balance of trade ❞

A country's *balance of trade* depends on the amount of its imports in relation to its exports. A country which exports more goods than it imports is said to have a *favourable balance* on its visible trade, because foreigners owe this country the money to pay for the surplus. On the other hand, a country where imports exceed exports is said to have an *adverse balance*, because it has to pay for the extra goods it imports. This calculation relates only to the visible items of trade.

Of course, a country such as Britain may make up its adverse balance on visible items by having a favourable balance on invisibles. With both taken into account it may finish in credit, with foreigners owing Britain more than Britain owes foreigners. This means that the total balance on current trading is favourable. If the invisible surplus is less than the visible deficit, it means that the total balance is adverse, but less adverse than it would have been.

Overseas investments

If a country continues in surplus, as Britain did for many years in the nineteenth century, this means that we build up a credit balance overseas. The sums left with foreigners abroad are known as *overseas investments*, and interest on these unpaid debts is due to Britain each year. These interest payments may take the form of goods, such as beef from Argentina, and so are the equivalent of an invisible export. Payments into the *capital account* (see page 57) balance the surplus in the current account, and transfers from the capital account make good any deficits in the current account – just as they do in the bank account of any private individual. These figures together form a country's *balance of payments*.

CHAPTER THREE COMMON PROBLEMS WITH STATISTICS

TERMS OF TRADE

..and the terms of trade

A country's *terms of trade* depend not on the volume of its trade, but on the value. If a country exports expensive electrical equipment overseas, the demand for which forces up the price, whilst importing cheap commodities like coffee, whose oversupply forces down the price, the country will be trading on favourable terms. As time goes by, it will be able to buy more in return for selling less, i.e. its terms of trade will be improving.

Conversely, a country has deteriorating terms of trade if its exports are declining in value through foreign competition, whilst its imports are becoming scarcer because of shortage of competing demands for supplies. Much of Britain's commercial strength in the nineteenth century arose from the fact that Britain was a monopoly supplier of manufactures at that time, and foreigners were forced to buy here, whilst the goods they sent in exchange were plentiful and were generally offered at a very low price.

At the same time, the more favourable our terms of trade, the more expensive are our exports, and this makes it hard for us to sell them. The more unfavourable the terms of trade, the more readily are we able to dispose of our goods to foreigners.

Terms of trade are generally reckoned as a *ratio* between two indices: the index of the price of exports over the index of the price of imports. In the base year, therefore, the terms of trade will stand at 1: $\frac{100}{100} = 1$

Improving terms of trade, then, produce a figure which is grater than 1, because the top figure is bigger than the bottom one. Deteriorating terms of trade produce a figure which is less than 1, because the bottom figure is bigger than the one on top. A country in an unfavourable trading position constantly has to increase its *volume* of exports to make good their falling *worth*.

BALANCE OF PAYMENTS

The balance of payments

Much of the information given above is expressed in the case of a given country in the form of a table which is known as the *balance of payments* table for that country. Here, the items on current account are separated into visibles and invisibles, and the current account is separated from the capital account. For Britain, the table is expressed in sterling, and therefore does not take into account the changes in the value of money. Let us take a simplified example:

Current Balance	1924	1931	1938	Current Balance	1924	1931	1938
Visible trade				Invisible trade			
Imports (−)	1291	870	939	Net shipping receipts	140	80	100
Exports (+)	953	462	562	Overseas investments	220	170	200
Balance on visible trade	−338	−408	−377	Commission charges	60	30	35
				Government transactions	−10	−24	−3
				Balance on current account	72	−104	−45

After the current account part of the table there follows the capital account which takes into account payments made in gold (− for imports, + for exports), new loans made (−), repayments (+), short-term capital movements (− for imports, + for exports), and quite a large residual figure resulting from transactions not recorded. The bottom part of the table balances the top part.

Capital Account	1924	1931	1938
Net gold movements	−1	31	204
New capital issues	−134	−41	−29
Repayments	−	42	69
Short-term capital movements	−	−91	−72
Residual payments	+63	163	−127

In the first column we see that in 1924 Britain had an overall surplus on current account of £72m. Imports of gold to the tune of £1m reduced this surplus to £71m, and Britain issued new loans amounting to this figure (actually £134m of new loans, less £63m of unspecified credits). Work out the other columns for yourself, remembering that Britain started in both the other years quoted with a deficit. The figures are only approximations, and this fact together with the very large residual figure, reduces the value of the statistics; but nevertheless, Britain can be seen by the end of the period to be losing its gold abroad very rapidly. N.B. 'Loss' of gold does not actually mean that it was packed into crates and physically shipped abroad. It merely means that the title of ownership to those amounts of gold was transferred to others, even though the gold itself remained in the same place. Supplies of gold are changed in other ways also. New gold is constantly being added all the time to the supply through mining, whilst gold is being withdrawn, for ornaments, dentistry and other non-monetary uses.

Figures such as these give a good overall idea of the position of a given country in the world economy. In many tables you will find them broken down into finer detail, but the outline above is sufficient to explain the main features of Britain's trading position during the inter-war years.

CHAPTER 4

PREPARING AND PRESENTING A COURSEWORK ASSIGNMENT

We will now trace the stages involved in successfully completing two pieces of coursework for GCSE Economic and Social History. Firstly, let us take the following assignment:

UNIT 1 STUDY ON INDUSTRIAL CHANGE

Question

Account for the increasing pace of industrial change in Britain during the 1780s and 1790s. Word limit 1500 words.

This exercise is *unstructured*, that is to say it is not split into separate parts. This makes it more difficult, and although structured exercises are more common in GCSE, it might be helpful to show you how to tackle an exercise of this sort first, and look at a structured exercise later.

The first pitfall to avoid occurs in the first two words. Account *for* does not mean the same thing as give an account *of*. Account for tests causation and is specifically asking for reasons, while giving an account of is simply narration. So you should recognise that the first skill in this exercise relates to *cause*. You may think that cause is the only skill, but look again. You are required to explain *industrial change*, so recognition and explanation of *change* is a second skill required. And there is a third; you are required to look at the *increasing pace* of industrial change, so you are not only looking at change, but also taking into account the speeding up of change in order to arrive at the appropriate causes. Another hidden skill arises from the unstructured nature of the exercise. You are not expected to produce a series of separate and unconnected causes. Part of the skill lies in seeing how causes are linked, and demonstrating this in your assignment so that an effective 'web' of causes emerges. It would be best therefore to collect material first, and then give careful thought to its order and arrangement, all the while bearing in mind that *causation*, not *narration*, is required and that *accelerating change* must be central to the argument.

1.1 Planning

You will need to do some background reading before you can tackle this assignment effectively. No book is likely to deal with this specific question head-on, but any book discussing the causes of industrial change is likely to contain material for you to work on. Thus you might consult the appropriate chapters in:

B. Turner, *GCSE British Social and Economic History* (Longman Revise Guide 1989), Chapters 2, 3, 5 and 6.

Other useful information might be found in:

C. P. Hill, *British Economic and Social History* (Arnold fourth edition 1977), Chapters 1–9 and Chapter 11.

P. Gregg, *A Social and Economic History of Britain* 1760–1972 (Harrap, 7th edition 1973), Chapter 2.

You may have access to other economic and social histories in your school or school library, such as those by Flynn or by Southgate. A lot of useful statistics and diagrams are to be found in E. J. Hobsbawm, *Industry and Empire* (Pelican Books 1968), but you will find most of that text too difficult to handle at this stage in your historical studies. Specialist books on transport, textiles and the iron industry could be useful for reference, provided that you remember that you are not only looking for the causes of industrial change, but those specific to the 1780s and 1790s which speeded up change.

So let us suppose that you have gathered a small selection of books, some borrowed from the local library, some readily available to you as textbooks. Your first task is to read and take notes from them in order to accumulate a useful body of relevant material. Remember that the focus of your interest should be on:

▶ the causes of industrial change
▶ the pace of industrial change
▶ the relevant period of the 1780s and 1790s.

If you group your notes on these features you will not drift too far away from the relevant focus so necessary to an effective piece of work.

1.2 Preparation

It should not be too difficult to accumulate *general* reasons for eighteenth-century industrial change. The Longman Revise Guide (*GCSE in Social and Economic History*) for example will tell you that in industrial terms Britain was already an advanced country by the *beginning* of the eighteenth century, thus getting a head start on possible industrial rivals. You will also be made aware of the rapid acceleration of population growth in the eighteenth century, increasing both the demand for goods and the supply of labour. Additionally, there were the efforts of successive governments, particularly those of Robert Walpole, Henry Pelham and the Younger Pitt to create the right political conditions for economic growth and prosperity. But there is a danger in setting off too soon.

```
The increasing pace of eighteenth-century industrial change is in part due
to the enormous population growth during the period: the population doubled
during the century, thus providing extra demand for manufactured products,
and extra labour to help make them. Britain already had an industrial edge
over other countries: even France had a much lower per capita output in 1700
than Britain, and Britain's governments provided the right economic
conditions with low taxation and low interest rates so that money was cheap
to borrow and therefore readily available for investment. Roads, though
bad, were better than those on the continent, and the spread of canals
facilitated the provision of consumer goods to the markets in the growing
towns.
```

While this appears to be on target, and certainly shows maturity of style, you will have noticed that this is generalised and not specific to the 1780s and 1790s. Let us see if we can improve it:

```
... population growth, which is generally agreed to have accelerated
sharply from about 1780. This obviously would not have immediately
increased the labour force, but it would be having an effect on labour
supply by the 1790s, and it would have had a fairly instant effect on demand
for goods, thus contributing to industrial growth. Britain ... than Britain
and in the Seven Years' War which ended in 1763 French colonies had been
captured by the British, and French commerce driven from the world's seas.
Although France was able to recover, Britain was in an unchallengeable
commercial position by the mid-1760s, and the efforts of Britain's
manufacturers and traders to respond to the opportunities were delayed by
the uncertainties of the American War from 1775-83, but were revived and
consolidated by the specific commercial policies of the Younger Pitt during
the ten years of peace from 1783-93. During these years interest rates fell,
and profits from commerce and agricultural improvement were now available
to be invested in the higher risk and high profit areas of industry rather
than in the low interest no-risk attractions of government bonds. Roads ...
on the continent: turnpike trusts, which in the 1750s were being set up at
the rate of ten a year were, by the 1780s, increasing at more than 50 a year
and with them went road improvements sufficient to allow the establishment
of regular mailcoach services in 1784, which took mail and also competed
with the private coach services to carry passengers: needless to say many of
```

these passengers were probably businessmen. The coaches did not carry much
merchandise, but the canals did. Their popularity sprang from the success
of Brindley's Bridgewater Canal which within ten years of its completion in
1769 was making enormous profits for its sponsors, carrying coal from
Worsley to Manchester. It is not surprising that once the cheapness and
reliability of canal transport was recognised — it was much more efficient
than the roads in carrying bulky and fragile goods — canal building was seen
as the answer to most transport problems, particularly that of supplying
the consumer markets in the growing towns. Canals were started in large
numbers in the 1780s and soon became such an important national activity
that the 1790s are recognised as the period of 'canal mania' when
'navigators' toiled to cover the country with an essential network of
canals.

There is now a strong focus on the 1780s and 1790s, and the work is no longer a potted summary of the causes of the Industrial Revolution. It is now about 450 words in length, and there is a good deal of material yet to cover. You must be wondering about all those inventions which seem to be such an important part of the Industrial Revolution:

- Kay's Flying Shuttle 1733
- Hargreave's Spinning Jenny 1765
- Arkwright's Water Frame 1769
- Watt's Separate Condenser 1769
- Crompton's Mule 1779
- Watt's Patent for Rotary Motion 1781
- Bells' Cylindrical Printing Process for Calicoes 1783
- Cartwright's Power Loom 1784
- Cort's Puddling Process 1783–4
- Eli Whitney's Cotton Gin 1793

It is obvious that you cannot just list and describe these. If you went to considerable length and backed up your text with accurate diagrams you would not necessarily be furthering the explanation of increasing change in the 1780s and 1790s. All of these are interesting in themselves, but how did they *contribute* to change? There is some clue in the dates: you will notice that most of them are concentrated in the last third of the eighteenth century, and you will probably agree that apart from the Darbys' technique of smelting with coal instead of charcoal in 1709, no *major* invention has been omitted. But there is a danger in thinking that all these inventions were immediately taken up on a large scale, especially those of the 1780s and 1790s which would suit your argument best, so it would be wise to check the texts and sources to see what effects on industry they actually did have. You would then be able to write along these lines:

Most of the technological inventions of the eighteenth century did not
appear by chance, they arose out of necessity. In the cotton industry the
continuing shortage of spun yarn to satisfy the demands of the weavers was
aggravated by the invention of Kay's Flying Shuttle in 1733 which speeded up
the weaving process and placed even further demands upon the spinners. It is
not surprising that efforts were made from the 1730s onwards to enable
spinners to work several spindles at once, and it was not until 1779 that
the problem was largely overcome with Crompton's Mule which could produce
thread for both weft and warp that was even and strong. As it contained some
of the features of Hargreaves' Jenny, Hargreaves' patent prevented the
Mule's widespread adoption until after 1790, by which time Watt's
improvements to the steam engine enabled it to be worked by steam power.
Cartwright's Power Loom of 1784 was a necessary response to the advances in
spinning, although at first the huge increases in the demand for woollen
cloth, partly brought about by war from 1793, were satisfied by the handloom
weavers for most of whom the 1790s ushered in a period of great prosperity.
The cotton industry derived more immediate benefit from the cylindrical
printing of cotton cloth, invented in 1783, and which, within twenty years
had helped enormously to increase the output of cottons.
  In the iron industry while there was plenty of wood fuel for charcoal the
use of coal for smelting, demonstrated by the Darbys of Coalbrookdale in
1709, was neglected. But shortages of wood, made worse by war demands in the
1760s, 1770s and early 1780s, led to smelting operations being fuelled by
coal instead of charcoal. As it was necessary to blast off the impurities

given off by burning coal it became increasingly economic to build large furnaces. During the 1790s the annual output of 'pig' iron more than doubled, and demand for it rose, especially when huge iron constructions such as the bridge over the Severn at Coalbrookdale, completed in 1781, showed that iron was not only a metal for swords, ploughshares and nails. Cort's 'puddling' process of the early 1780s, although it brought Cort poverty and dishonour, was soon adopted by others, and more plentiful supplies of 'wrought' iron helped to create its own demand; its ready availability, cheapness and lasting qualities made it the perfect medium for the new engineering which was to develop from Watt's improved engines and the new textile inventions. Iron production and the use of steam power enormously increased the demand for coal. The old 'open-cast' and 'adit' mines could not meet it and deeper mines had to be dug. By the 1780s 140 of Newcomen's engines, with improvements by Watt, were pumping water out of deeper mines. By the 1790s winding gear was being introduced into the larger pits; iron rails, introduced in 1767, were commonplace in pits by the 1790s. All this was necessary if the mines were to increase output, and indeed production quadrupled during the eighteenth century, most of the increase coming in the last quarter of the century.

Here, there is an attempt to link the inventions with industrial change, and although modern research would suggest the need for some caution on the immediate impact of technological change, the picture given is reasonable enough. You may have realised that the 1500 words target has almost been reached, and as the text is not yet complete there will be need for further editing and rearranging. Your reading and notes will surely suggest that the 1790s saw the beginning of the long period of European warfare against revolutionary France. How did that affect Britain's pace of change? The preoccupation of Europe with warfare ought to have stimulated industrial competition there. The main demand was for ships, iron for artillery and small arms, and textiles for uniforms. And there was also an insatiable demand for capital to finance huge war expenditure. You ought to be able to make use of these basic ideas.

The war which began in 1793 gave a further impetus to industry. Not only did the needs of war enormously increase demand for armaments and ships, but also textiles for uniforms and leather for boots. Oddly enough Britain found itself supplying its enemies with some of these commodities, because Britain was the only country capable of supplying iron and textiles in the vast quantities now required. To meet the demand manufacturers needed capital to introduce new technology and factory methods of production: although capital was a scarce resource, at least profits from agricultural improvement and returns from canal investment (the 'canal mania' was slowing down by the mid-1790s, so canals became a producer of capital rather than a consumer of it) were able largely to finance the industrial change which in most other countries ground to a halt because of war. The agricultural revolution provided leather for the boot and shoe industry, and the war demand helped create a mass-produced product in an industry which until the late eighteenth century had been virtually exclusively a 'craft' industry.

1.3 Completing the writing

The word limit is getting close and thought has to be given to the arrangement and order so that you can produce a 'web of causation'. It is also necessary to consider whether there is sufficient evidence to show an 'increased pace of change', or whether the idea of the rapid acceleration of the industrial revolution in the late eighteenth century needs to be modified. Are there any major themes still omitted, and is it relevant to include reference to the lack of 'limited liability' and the profusion of small, vulnerable banks which probably hindered rather than hastened industrial development? Perhaps these latter points could qualify the text in the appropriate places, and it would be better to have a look at the order of argument. As it stands at present the points are presented in this sequence:

1 Population growth – labour supply and demand
2 Britain's industrial edge over other countries
3 The Seven Years War impetus; War of American Independence setback
4 Pitt's policies
5 Availability of capital
6 Transport – roads and canals

7   Textile industry – the Mule, power loom, cylindrical printing
8   Iron industry – coal, blast furnaces, puddling, demand, steam power, coal mines
9   War – demand, capital, shoe industry.

This contains nine main themes with sub-developments. Are they in a logical order? 'Demand' appears twice, 'capital' appears twice, wars are dealt with in two places. As point 2 has not a direct chronological relevance it might be better as introduction. If population growth is dealt with next this would lead directly to demand and thus to points 3 and 9 on war. Pitt's inter-war financial policies (4) would then follow on logically, with its effect on 5. The interlinking changes of 6, 7 and 8 could probably be dealt with in that order with a little more flexibility and freedom.

Having decided on a final order, the best thing to do is to try it out and write up the finished version, being prepared to make changes if necessary during the course of the writing. Compare this version with the earlier drafts in this chapter, and see if you can understand the reasons for the changes you notice and approve them. Some of them are second thoughts and additional thoughts of the kind that should occur to you as you get your drafts into final form.

Many of the favourable factors which led to the industrial revolution in Britain existed in other European countries, and the technological changes needed were simple rather than complex, and well within the capabilities of eighteenth century man. Yet as early as the beginning of the century Britain had an industrial edge over other countries, and even France had a lower output per head than Britain. But industrial change was slow to take off, and while Britain's population increased only slowly as it did throughout most of the eighteenth century, there seemed no need for and little possibility of dramatic industrial change.

However, there is no doubt that the last quarter of the eighteenth century was the period of most of the change that doubled Britain's population between 1700 and 1800. The sharp acceleration from about 1780 not only helped to stimulate agricultural change, in order to meet demands for food, but created a demand for consumer products, especially textiles, which existing manufacturing methods were unable to satisfy. By the 1790s this population increase was not only stimulating demand, but was also now beginning to contribute to an expanding labour supply without which there could be no effective industrial growth.

The demands of the growing population coincided with increased demand brought about by war. The Seven Years War (1756–63) and the War of American Independence (1775–83) stimulated both the iron and the textile industries with their need for guns, swords and uniforms. The Seven Years War increased Britain's colonies, and thus markets, at France's expense, and drove French commerce from the world's seas. Although France was able to make partial recovery, Britain gained an unchallengeable commercial position by the mid-1760s, and the efforts of Britain's manufacturers and traders to respond to the opportunities, although delayed by the American War, were to redouble from the mid-1780s. The Revolutionary wars which began in 1793 gave a further impetus to industry. War supplies were needed on a much larger scale than in either of the previous wars, as both France and its coalition enemies raised armies on a scale never before seen. Oddly enough Britain found itself supplying iron, textiles and footwear to the enemy, because Britain was the only country able to provide the huge quantities now required. War disrupted the ability of Continental countries to undergo largescale industrial change, but war stimulated Britain's ability to do so.

While France and its allies committed their limited capital resources to war, Britain had enough capital to fight and to industrialise. That Britain was able to do so was due in no small measure to the excellence of its financial institutions and the skill of its politicians. Walpole and Pelham laid secure financial and commercial foundations, aided by one of the most advanced banking systems in Europe. The steadying influence of a National Bank, the Bank of England, founded in 1694, had no parallel in France (except for a brief failure in 1719–20) until 1808. If the American war caused a temporary financial hiccough, Pitt's policy of peace, financial reform and the favourable trade treaty with France in 1785, revived financial and commercial confidence and boosted trade. In particular the confidence inspired low interest rates, and these encouraged investment in the higher risk and high profit areas of industry and transport, rather than in the low-interest, no-risk attractions of government bonds.

It might be queried where the investment capital was coming from if Pitt needed to borrow heavily for war. But Pitt enjoyed ten years of peace from 1783-93. Increasing profits from commerce and agriculture flowed into industry and particularly during the 1780s into canal construction. By the time that the war began in 1793 the 'canal mania' was largely over and canals became providers of capital rather than consumers of it.

The heavy investment in canals in the 1780s and 1790s was vital as a catalyst to industrial change. Their popularity sprang from the success of Brindley's Bridgewater Canal which within ten years of its completion in 1769 was making enormous profits for its sponsors carrying coal from Worsley to Manchester. It is not surprising that once the cheapness and reliability of canal transport was recognised — it was much more efficient than the roads in carrying bulky and fragile goods — canal-building was seen as the answer to most transport problems, particularly that of supplying the consumer markets in the growing towns. Canals were started in large numbers in the 1780s and soon became such an important national activity that the late 1780s and early 1790s are recognised as the period of the 'canal mania' when 'navigators' toiled to cover the country with an essential network of canals. Of course canals could not be built everywhere, and road improvements were the canals' essential partner. As early as the 1750s turnpike trusts were being set up at the rate of ten a year. By the 1780s this had increased to 50 a year, and road improvements were such that regular passenger coach services were connecting the major towns with increasing frequency, and having to compete with the regular mail coach services established in 1784. Businessmen used the coaches to tout personally for business, used the canals to transport their goods, and used the mail (and the 1d and 2d mail in London from the 1780s) to receive orders and maintain business contacts.

But if industry was looking for more orders, it had to have the capacity to satisfy both the insatiable demands of warring governments and those of the new consumers. Greater capacity required technological change. Most of the technological inventions of the eighteenth century did not appear by chance, they arose out of necessity. In the cotton industry the continuing shortage of spun yarn to satisfy the demands of the weavers was aggravated by the invention of Kay's Flying Shuttle in 1733 which speeded up the weaving process and placed even further demands upon the spinners. It is not surprising that efforts were soon made to provide the technology for spinners to work several spindles at once, but it was not until 1779 that the problem was largely overcome with Crompton's Mule. The Mule was widely adopted in the cotton industry from the 1790s onwards, by which time Watt's improvements to the steam engine enabled it to be worked by steam power. Cartwright's Power Loom of 1784 was a necessary response to the advances in spinning and both Mule and Power Loom necessitated the change from cottage and workshop to factory, as did Eli Whitney's Cotton Gin of 1793. So the greatest single change in industrial organisation was made possible by inventions that came into use in the 1780s and 1790s. The cotton industry was further boosted by the invention of cylindrical printing in 1783; this enormously reduced the price of coloured cottons, boosted demand for them, and within twenty years led to an enormous increase in output.

These textile changes had their parallels in the iron industry. Although the Darbys of Coalbrookdale had demonstrated the smelting of iron ore with coal as early as 1709, it was not until the 1780s, with increasing shortages and rocketing prices of wood fuel, that smelting with coal was widely adopted. The necessity in this process of blasting off the impurities from the coal made small furnaces uneconomic, especially as 'blasting' required much higher temperatures, and large furnaces became standard. During the 1790s the output of 'pig iron' more than doubled, and demand for it rose, especially when huge iron constructions such as the bridge over the Severn at Coalbrookdale, completed in 1781, showed that iron was not only a metal for swords, ploughshares and nails. A huge expansion in the output of iron was assured when Cort's 'puddling' process of the early 1780s applied coal to the manufacture of wrought iron, and the new engineering, made possible by Watt's steam engines and stimulated by the textile inventions which could employ steam power, ensured a rapidly rising market for an expanding industry. All this activity necessitated an expanding coal industry. The old 'open-cast' and 'adit' mines could not meet the demand, and deeper mines had to be dug. By the 1780s 140 of Newcomen's engines, with improvements by Watt, were pumping water out of deeper mines. By the 1790s winding gear was being installed in the larger pits; iron rails, introduced in 1767, were commonplace in pits before the end of the century. Coal production quadrupled between 1700 and 1800, most of the increase coming in the last twenty years of the century.

The 1780s and 1790s were years of growing demand stimulated by a rising population and war, and were years of increased output stimulated by technological change and transport improvements. The beginnings of the factory system, and the widening of industrial markets from local to national date from this period. It was not entirely a smooth transition; war rewarded handloom weavers as well as factory owners, and war made capital more expensive and investment more difficult. But in the transition from an agricultural economy to the 'workshop of the world' these two decades contain a combination of so many of the contributory factors which gave the impetus to dramatic change.

1.4 Examiner's mark scheme

On an assignment of this kind the examiner will set out his mark scheme in the form of the various *levels of achievement*. There may be up to four or five levels, and in all cases except where very brief answers are required there will be at least three.

Target: Causation, continuity and change

Level 1: scattered factual material *(1–4)*
Level 2: a narrative treatment from which causes of change do emerge *(5–8)*
Level 3: reasons for industrial change listed *(9–12)*
Level 4: good treatment of the causes of change, with either a 'web' of causation or an attempt to focus on the 'pace' of change *(13–17)*
Level 5: the answer combines a 'web' of causation with some attempt to convey the idea of the 'pace' of change *(18–20)*

> How well did we do?

Try to work out for yourself how highly the final draft above would have fared under this scheme. You ought to be prepared to place it in Level 5. Can you see why?

UNIT 2 — STUDY USING DOCUMENTARY SOURCES

There is no doubt that the most popular parts of the Social and Economic course occur near the beginning. Candidates seem to prefer tackling questions on the eighteenth century – on the agrarian, industrial and transport revolutions – than on the economic and social developments of the twentieth century. So it does not seem unreasonable to follow the question on the Industrial Revolution with one on the Agricultural (or Agrarian) Revolution. There are plenty of examples of student work of differing quality on many other themes of the syllabus, both nineteenth and twentieth century, in Chapter 5. Here we shall tackle a sources question on the Agricultural Revolution. Remember from Chapter 1 that different Boards have rather different aims and approaches; in this example the aim is to show high sources skills in most sub-questions and conclude with a sub-question requiring empathy. The sources themselves should provide considerable help in developing an empathetic answer. Look carefully at the mark tariffs with each sub-question to decide how much you need to write.

> A documentary assignment

Study sources A to G below, and then answer questions a) to d) which follow.

Source A

Oath of an Enclosure Commissioner, 1792.

I William Hill do swear that I will faithfully, impartially and honestly, according to the best of my skill and judgment execute the trusts imposed in me as a Commissioner by virtue of an Act of Parliament for dividing and enclosing the several open Common Moors and Waste Grounds within the Manor and Township of Ecclesall in the Parish of Sheffield in the West Riding of the County of York without favour

or affection to any person or persons whomsoever,
So help me God,
William Hill

(Quoted in John Addy, *The Agrarian Revolution*, Longman)

Source B

After the Enclosure Bill was passed the commissioners took over. Far from being appointed as guardians of the interests of the small landowners threatened by enclosure, these consisted of a representative of the lord of the manor (until 1801 the lord himself could act as a Commissioner), a representative of the majority – *in value*, not in *numbers* – of the owners. These Commissioners ... thus represented the very people who had introduced the Enclosure Bill.

(Adapted from Pauline Gregg, *A Social and Economic History of Britain, 1760–1972*, Harrap.)

Source C

A poet's view of the effects of enclosure.

Ill fares the land, to hastening ills a prey,
Where wealth accumulates, and men decay;
Princes and lords may flourish, or may fade.
A breath can make them, as a breath has made;
But a cold peasantry, their country's pride,
When once destroyed, can never be supplied.

(from Oliver Goldsmith, *The Deserted Village, 1769*)

Source D

Arthur Young's views on the effect of enclosure upon the poor.

I will not dispute the good intentions of the enclosures; but the poor look to facts, not intentions; and the fact is, that by nineteen enclosure bills in twenty they are injured, in some grossly injured. It may be said that commissioners are sworn to do justice. What is that to people who suffer? It must be generally known that they suffer in their own opinions, and yet enclosures go on by commissioners, who dissipate the poor people's cows wherever they come, as well those kept legally as those which are not. What is it to the poor man to be told that the Houses of Parliament are extremely tender of property, while the father of the family is forced to sell his cow and his land ... and being deprived of the only motive to industry, squanders the money, contracts bad habits, enlists as a soldier, and leaves the wife and children to the parish? If enclosures were beneficial to the poor, rates would not rise as in other parishes after an act to enclose. The poor in these parishes may say, and with truth ... all I know is, I had a cow, and an Act of Parliament has taken it from me.

(Adapted from Arthur Young, *An Inquiry into the Propriety of Applying Wastes etc. 1801*)

Source E

Estimated annual national expenditure on Poor Relief.

   1760   £1 000 000
   1780   £1 800 000
   1800   £3 500 000
   1820   £7 500 000

(by extrapolation from various sources)

Source F

An historian's view of the effects of enclosure.

While the large landed proprietors and the wealthy tenant and yeomen farmers benefited considerably from enclosure, the position of the majority of the villagers, particularly the poorer classes, became materially worse. They had been allowed to pasture a cow, and perhaps a few sheep, pigs, and poultry, on the commons and wastes, although they had no legal claim to do so. They enjoyed this right because it was the custom of the village. When the commons were enclosed, they lost this privilege, and even when they were given small pieces of land in exchange, these did not adequately compensate them for their loss. Sometimes a piece of common perhaps twenty to forty acres in extent was set aside by the commissioners for the use of the poor, but generally the villagers who eked out their small weekly wages by keeping a little stock, became landless labourers, dependent solely on their wages. The small yeomen and copyholders, who held perhaps ten to thirty acres, were also injured by the loss of common rights. In addition, they had to bear their share of the expenses of enclosure and of fencing their land, the latter alone costing three to five pounds an acre. As few of them had any money, they had either to mortgage or sell their land. Some of them became tenant farmers, using the proceeds of the sale to rent and stock bigger farms, while others went to the towns or became landless labourers.

(Adapted from D. W. Roberts, *An Outline of the Economic History of England*, Longman, first published as a school textbook, 1931, revised 1940)

Source G

The views of another historian.

The case for enclosure was that it enabled uncultivated land to be brought into use and made the commercially-minded 'improving' farmer independent of his more custom-bound and old-fashioned neighbours. This was undoubtedly so. The case against it is by no means clear, because its opponents have only too often confused the specific device of the Enclosure Act with the general phenomenon of agricultural concentration of which it was only one aspect. It was accused of throwing peasants off their holdings and labourers out of work. The second charge was true where enclosure transformed former tilled fields into pastures, which happened sometimes, but – in view of the booming demand for corn, especially during the Napoleonic Wars – by no means generally. Enclosure for tillage, or from uncultivated land, might actually mean more local work. How far enclosure acts threw small cultivators off the land is a matter of debate, but there is no reason to suppose that they did so any more effectively than the buying out or leasing of strips and smallholdings in earlier periods.

(Adapted from E. J. Hobsbawm, *Industry and Empire*, Weidenfeld and Nicolson, 1968, Volume 3 of the Pelican Economic History of Britain)

a) Consult sources A, B, D and F. How good and adequate a safeguard was the oath taken by the Enclosure commissioners, as a guarantee that they would do their job as fairly as possible? (4 marks)
b) How far are sources C and D in agreement? Which of the two is likely to be the more reliable source, and why? How effectively do the statistics in source E support the argument of source D? (6 marks)
c) Consult sources F and G. In what ways do the two sources differ? Which source do you think is likely to give a more accurate picture of the effects of enclosure? Give reasons for your answer. (5 marks)
d) Explain how villagers at a public meeting towards the end of the eighteenth century might have reacted to local proposals for enclosure. You may make use of the sources, and you may consult other sources if you wish. (10 marks)

Your answers should not exceed a total of 1000 words.

2.1 Planning and preparation

The instruction to *study the sources* at the start of the assignment means that you must spend some time examining them before attempting any of the questions. It is likely that you will already be generally familiar with the Agricultural Revolution and that you will have studied the appropriate sections of some of the texts mentioned as reading for the first assignment. In addition you might dip into or use for reference one of the more specialist books on the Agricultural Revolution such as Chambers and Mingay, *The Agricultural Revolution, 1750–1880*, Batsford 1966. Although this book is written for more advanced students, much of it is straightforward enough for good GCSE students to understand, even if the *detail* is more than required for GCSE. Remember, too, that the questions do not forbid you to use outside information; in fact d) actually encourages you to do so. Thus you might not only make some general notes on the reasons for, and the effects of, enclosure from your own reading, you might also look up important figures like Arthur Young and Oliver Goldsmith to see if further information about them will help your analysis of the sources.

Then, too, the sources themselves will need careful reading and study. You must read them slowly through, making sure that you understand them and you must look up words that you don't understand such as *impartially, phenomenon* and *beneficial*, and technical words like *leasehold, mortgage, tillage*. You may find it difficult to get a word by word meaning of Goldsmith's poem, but you ought to get the general overall idea of it, and you could ask for help if an insuperable problem arose with it. If complex sentences appear in the texts you must be sure to unravel them, so that you know exactly what each source means.

Next you must study the sub-questions and the mark tariff allowed for each. The answers to a), b) and c) will be similar in length, although 6 marks suggests that b) could be a little more weighty. For d), however, the 10 mark allocation requiring empathetic skills suggests a more extended answer than those of a) to c) which are concerned with comparison and evaluation of sources. In answering all these sub-questions particular care must be taken not to duplicate or overlap the answer material, so that your answers will not be repetitive.

2.2 Completing the writing

All the extracts are dealing specifically, or by implication, with the effects of enclosure. You may argue that the statistics are about relief of the poor, but you have to judge whether these statistics support an assertion about the link between enclosure and poverty.

In tackling a) you will notice the solemn oath, the allegations in b) and the references in d) and f). From your reading you should be aware that the commissioner had no option about what procedures to adopt and what interpretations to make; these were clearly laid down by parliament, and that where he was able to take decisions – i.e. in the reallocation of land – he had a task that was almost impossible to do fairly. This should help temper assumptions that might otherwise have been made purely on the textual evidence presented here.

a) In an age when religious belief was strong and religious observance fairly universal, an oath, taken in the sight of God was not to be taken lightly. It is unlikely that the vast majority of commissioners took such an oath with every or any intention of breaking it. There is evidence that they carried out their work with care, trying to distribute the land fairly between landowners and being scrupulous about allocating commons where the act required it, as suggested in F. But with the best will in the world the commissioners, themselves important landowners, could hardly avoid being motivated, if only unconsciously, by some element of self-interest. If the lord of the manor and the most important landowners were commissioners, their motives and actions would be suspect, no matter how good their intentions.

You need to check whether the two sources C and D are in fact on the same track; you may well feel that they are suggesting two different results of enclosure – the destruction of a class and poverty. You should compare the credentials of the two authors as specialists on the rural scene, and you should be aware of the limitations as well as the value of statistics.

b) Despite its title this excerpt from Goldsmith's poem is not specifically dealing with rural depopulation, it is dealing with the destruction of the peasant class, while Young deals with rural poverty. Goldsmith's is an emotional outcry in which accuracy is less important than the poetry itself. Young, however, was a progressive farmer for whom enclosure was the road to agricultural improvement. How much more convincing then, his attack on this aspect of the cause to which he was committed. There is little evidence to support the notion of widespread 'deserted villages' and 'decayed peasantry' (compare with source G), but Young's observations ring true, especially when it is remembered that the Enclosures Acts carefully distinguished between 'rights' and 'custom' (cf. source F). The statistics in source E should be treated with caution. They may support Young's argument in D, but there is no guarantee that the years chosen are not freak years, there could be significant changes in the value of money not taken into account, and a large population growth could in itself account for extra spending on poverty. Extrapolated statistics may well be rather unreliable. Perhaps, too, a greater sense of social justice led to greater spending on poor relief. Even so, the trend shown in the statistics does seem to add some corroboration to Young's views.

In looking at c) you should compare both texts closely for similarity and difference and then try to explain the differences. Look at the dates of publication. Look at the purpose for which the books were written, and see if you can find out anything about the authors.

c) The difference in the texts is not merely one of content. F is written in narrative style. It lists the sufferings of villagers under enclosure, and implies some rural depopulation in its last sentence. G, on the other hand, is developing an argument and seems to be attacking the views of earlier historians. Hobsbawm certainly queries general rural depopulation, and suggests that even the general dispossession of peasants has been exaggerated. Roberts's book was intended as a text book for schools, and attempted to simplify for the purpose historical knowledge and scholarship as it stood at that time. He does not appear to have had Hobsbawm's high academic standing, and he was, moreover, writing nearly thirty years before Hobsbawm. Hobsbawm's book seems to have been aimed at a more sophisticated audience. In the absence of other evidence and in view of Hobsbawm's academic reputation it would seem safer to prefer G.

The last part of this assignment is empathetic, and carries the highest marks. It is obvious that if the villagers have only one standard attitude to the proposed enclosure then the result could only be stereotyped empathy reaching Level 2 at most. Is it any better if the villagers are divided into several groups and collective views attributed to each? Thus we could have wealthy landowners, tenant farmers, small-holders, and labourers or cottagers. With landowners in favour and all the other groups against, surely that would be differentiated empathy? But in fact what would result would be a series of stereotyped groups, when the best approach would be to cater for differing opinions *within* groups, not forgetting to make use of the source material. It is vitally important to remember than in empathetic work *any* any kind of stereotyping should be avoided, and that the best way to do this is to have people within an obvious group expressing clearly differing opinions.

d) At the meeting several landowners who held nearly half the manor between them spent much time putting forward the case for enclosure; that it was the only way to agricultural improvement, and that the present system held back the introduction of new methods. They cited the incidence of cattle disease on the common lands and the overgrazing, and they condemned the strip system as time-wasting and inefficient. One major landowner, however, was not easily convinced. He was worried that separate plots would mean labour shortages in busy seasons like the harvest and ploughing, and he was not keen to lose land his family had nurtured for centuries in exchange for land that had been badly cared for by some of his idle neighbours. Tenant farmers were worried generally about the security of their leases under enclosure, but most of them supported it for the opportunities it would give them, despite reservations about enclosure costs and legal fees. Some of the small-holders shared these misgivings and were anxious too about how a large field of uneven quality could be redistributed fairly. It would be easy to give a large landowner a cross-section of differing quality land, but a man allocated 5% of a field might have to put up with a piece of poor quality land, and compensating him with extra acreage would merely add to his costs rather than to his assets. Even so other smallholders welcomed the prospect of being able to make their own decisions of what to grow and when to grow it, or even of the possibility of converting to pastoral farming and stockbreeding. The vicar was worried that the social unity of the village would be broken up and the caring communal spirit of co-operation would be lost for ever. The most concerned were the landless labourers and cottagers who were alarmed at the loss of their common and grazing rights and feared that if there was much enclosure of tillage for pasture there would be no employment for them. But several labourers thought that with agricultural improvement following enclosure the richer farmers would be able to employ more men and increase wages, so that perhaps enclosure would not be such a disaster after all. On a show of hands the owners of more than 50% of the land seemed to be in favour of enclosure, so it seems that the local Enclosure Act will succeed as few of its opponents can afford the legal expense of fighting it.

2.3 Examiner's mark scheme

a) to c) are concerned with source skills, and would be assessed as follows:

Level 1: Comprehension of source – candidate can extract information from sources and make simple deductions and inferences. *(1–5 marks)*

Level 2: Simple evaluation – candidate can classify the type of source, comment on the nature and tone of information provided, detect omissions and bias, and distinguish between fact and opinion. *(6–10 marks)*

Level 3: Supported evaluation – candidate can evaluate the source by a general sense of period, in terms of the author's situation or purpose, or by a process of cross-referencing (comparing one source with another); uses sources as evidence rather than information, and can draw reasoned historical conclusions.
(11–15 marks)

You should be able to see that there is enough in answers a) to c) to place the mark at the top end of Level 3.

For d) there is the usual empathy mark scheme:

Level 1: Everyday empathy; either vague generalisations about the past, or typically modern ideas and motives are attributed to people in the past. *(1–3 marks)*

Level 2: Stereotyped historical empathy; candidate realises that people in the past had different ideas about the world from people in the present, but assumes that people in the past thought the same way about specific issues. *(4–6 marks)*

Level 3: Differentiated empathy; candidate realises that not only did people in the past think differently from those in the present, but recognises that these ideas will not be uniformly held. The answer shows that different views were held by different groups and by different individuals within groups. *(7–10 marks)*

You should be able to recognise that the answer to d) meets the requirements of Level 3 and should gain a high mark within that Level.

CHAPTER 5

EXAMPLES OF STUDENTS' COURSEWORK

Study each of these examples carefully

This chapter is made up of a number of actual examples of pieces of coursework produced by students. They cover the range of skills required in coursework, especially assessment objectives 2, 3 and 4. Study each assignment carefully, and note which of the assessment objectives it is supposed to cover. Then read the student's work, and decide whether you think it:

- carries out the task set
- meets the necessary assessment objective(s)
- is a good example of what the student ought to be able to do.

Having made up your own mind about the quality of the work, then read and study the examiner's comments, given at the end of each assignment. How does your verdict compare with his? Congratulate yourself if you and he are in broad agreement. This shows you are thinking along the right lines, and have a good idea of what a piece of coursework should be like. If not, make sure you understand *why* you differ, and see if you can get closer to the examiner's thinking on the next example.

UNIT 1 INDUSTRIAL DEVELOPMENTS SINCE 1870

Assessment objective 1: Selection, development and communication of content

QUESTION

Explain, and show the importance of the changes that took place in British industry in the half-century after 1870.
You may include any of the following *or other material* in your answer:

i) new industries
ii) new forms of transport
iii) sources of power
iv) the effects of foreign competition.

1.1 The student's answer

In the fifty years after 1870 things got more modern. With the modernization of industry things got a lot better. Working conditions were pleasanter, and there was big increases in pay. More skills were needed as industry got more scientific and up-to-date. A lot of industrys grew, but others were forced to close down or to merge so as to acheeve higher degrees of eficiensy. In particular the stable trades were in decline like shipbuilding and coal mines. Many of these became redundent and the workers moved elsewhere. Even on the railways deesel locomotives began to be introduced to replace steam. Motorcars came into use and to computers were invented which made industry much better. It was also the age of the airoplane. Plastics began to be invented and manmade fibres like rayon began to be produced. In building there were now more concreete buildings, and concreete was also used on building the new motorways.

All this was very important because it helped to ease unemployment and inflation and ennabled Britain to prepare for the coming of the First World War in 1914.

i) New industrys came in for the first time. Motorcars came into use. It was also the age of the airoplane. Instead of the old stable industrys there were new industrys like plastics and manmade fibres such as rayon. The most important was the motorcar industry. There was also new processes within industry. The Bessimer converter was replaced by the open-hearth furnace and the electric furnace so that steel became cheaper and more plentiful. New processes were invented to further revolutionize the textile industry with new methods of spinning and weaving. All this helped to keep Britain in the fourfront of industrial advance.

ii) New forms of transport came in for the first time. Motorcars came into use and it was also the age of the airoplane. On the railways, deesel and deesel-electric began to replace steam power, and electric trains also came into wide use. The tram was invented and the penny-farthing bycicle. The most important was the motorcar industry. The first economically successful motorcar was built by Gottlieb Daimler in 1889. It arose out of his experience in manufacturing engines driven by the controled explosions of a mixture of air and coal gas. He decided to adapt such an engine to the propulsion of a light carridge, substituting petrol vapour for coal gas because liquid fuel could more easily be carried. Besides the motorcar, the internal combustion engine has given us the motocycle, with or without side-car, the autocycle, the taxi-cab, which will take you one mile or a hundred (if you can pay), the bus, the motor-van and the lorry. All these are very important and without them there would be nothing to put on the motorways.

iii) There were new sourses of power. The most important of these were petrol and oil, for driving the new forms of transport such as the motorcar. It was also the age of the airoplane, and high octave fuel was used to power the new flying airoplanes. The most important new fuel was electricity and gas. The gas came from the North Sea but most of the petrol was imported together with the oil from the rich oilfields of the Middle East. The dynamo was invented by Michael Faraday and came into wide uses after 1870. It was first of all driven by coal and steam, but later these were replaced by oil-driven generators, and in more recent times by nuclear power. This has been very controversial up to now and has not yet been settled.

iv) There was a good deal of foreign competition, especially in foreign motorcars. The Japanese produced very cheap and reliable cars, and these have to some extent made inroads into the British market. There are now even some Japanese companys in Britain making there cars here instead of in Japan. The main cause of this competition was that these countrys industrialized later than Britain so at first they were not much of a challange, but later it became more serious. Overall the fifty years after 1870 saw a good deal in the growth of foreign competition.

1.2 Examiner's comments

This is in fact an example of how *not* to tackle a piece of historical coursework. There is nothing to suggest even that the student has read the question properly. This form of question – which is not unusual in GCSE – takes the form of a general question, and then suggests *guidelines* for the answer. These are not compulsory; you may if you wish confine yourself to these in your answer; *or* you may include them, but bring in others as well; *or* you may ignore them, and refer in your answer to completely different things (this last course seems, however, rather reckless, since the guidelines are probably chosen for their appropriateness, not because they are peripheral).

This student has tackled them as if they were merely the a), b), c), d) of a normal structured question. The result is that instead of gaining the greater flexibility which this style of question is meant to confer, the student has employed it like a strait-jacket.

Nor is the written material offered of an acceptable standard. There is some use of style and language, but the spelling is inexcusably weak, the chronology insecure, and the presentation random and laughably repetitive. The phrase 'it was the age of the airoplane' (i.e. aeroplane) appears in almost all the subsections of the answer. Anachronisms (the placing of historical events in a sequence out of their proper time, i.e. too soon or too late for accuracy) occur abundantly, and there is a suggestion in ii) that the student has lifted a short passage about Daimler from a child's story book (note the giveaway phrase 'one mile or a hundred (if you can pay)').

The pattern followed by the answer takes the form of a generalized introduction, much of which is then repeated in the sub-sections of the answer. The style is a narrative one; although the student occasionally remembers about 'importance' he is rarely able to demonstrate it, or say anything useful about it. What importance there is often takes the form of a simple reassertion of the words in the question, e.g. 'Overall the fifty years after 1870 saw a good deal in the growth of foreign competition.' What would have been better would have been some specific and detailed information about the nature and extent of this competition and the *ways* in which it was important.

The anachronisms begin early in the piece; the decline of heavy ('staple', not 'stable') industry occurs mainly after 1920, rather than before that date; diesel locomotives did not replace steam until the 1960s; it could hardly be said to be 'the age of the plane' before 1920; rayon and plastics had to wait until the 1930s and later; there were no motorways until long after the Second World War; concrete was not yet in general use as a major building material, and computers had not yet been developed. Some of these errors are then repeated in (i) and (ii) – together with electric trains (possibly the student is really referring here to trams). In the answer to (iii), gas was a fuel long before 1870 (it was, in fact, one of the earliest), while nuclear power certainly had not yet made an appearance by 1920! The theme of foreign competition in (iv) is valid, but the student has very little to say about it, and the Japanese example he manages to dredge up is more appropriate to the late twentieth century rather than to the pre-1920 period.

The spelling throughout is poor. There may be some excuse for this in the stress of examination conditions; but there can be no excuse for it in coursework, where you can look up every word in the dictionary if you wish. Indeed, for those students with a known spelling weakness, it is a good idea to have a *dictionary* alongside you as you work.

There is no book-list (*bibliography*), and so it is impossible for the examiner to tell what books have been used for the assignment. In view of the thinness of the material and the errors built into the answer, a list of books would have been interesting; but the suspicion remains that no authorities at all were in fact consulted.

The whole piece is so inaccurately informed, and so lacking in any proper indication of the *importance of the changes* that it can score only the lowest of marks. To score better, the work would have to be better planned, better informed, better argued and better presented. In particular it would have to refer in greater detail to specific historical examples. Remember that one well-chosen example is more effective than a dozen badly-chosen ones. Work which repeats the same example has every appearance of intellectual poverty (perhaps in this case all too justified).

UNIT 2 — THE GENERAL STRIKE: A WORKING-CLASS REVOLUTION?

▶ Assessment objective 2: Cause and consequence

QUESTION

a) What factors led to the calling of a General Strike in Britain in May 1926? Why was the strike at first so widely supported by the workers?
b) Why did the strike make such a deep impression at the time?
c) What were the effects of the collapse of the General Strike on British labour history over the next twenty years?

2.1 The student's answer

a) The economic causes of the peace treatys were in the nature of boomerangs coming back to injure us. Two other factors added to our troubles. Britain had borrowed heavily from the USA, and she had used her credit to obtain goods for her allys, who's credit was not as high as hers. She was now bound to repay the money borrowed from the USA with interest, whilst as time passed her dettors seased to pay her. In addition, the demobbilization of the armys and the sessation of work on munitions, disloccated employment. Hundreds of thousand of munitions workers lost there jobs, while the returning soldiers failed to find work. The cost of living had doubled during the war and did not fall to it's original level, while employers wished to reduce wages from there very high war levels.

Modern developments hit most heavily what were once our stable industrys. Coal-mining and railways obviously suffered from the advance of the motorcar, from the substitution of oil for coal in the navy and in industry, and from the growing rise in the use of electricity. The miners threatened to strike and the government appointed a Comission to ennquire into there greevances, advocating that the State should take over the mines. This the Coalition government delayed to do.

The miners were soon suffering increasingly from the decline in coal, and were faced with reductions in there wages. The government subsidy was withdrawn. The mine-owners decided to lower wages or lengthen hours. Against this the miners struck and were soon supported by the other two great unions, the railwaymen and the dockers. All Labour rallied to their support and a General Strike was declared, May 1926. The strike was widely supported because most of the workers were in favour of it.

b) The strike made a deep impression because it was very important. This was the first time for many years that the coalminers had struck, and a lot of the ordinary people were bound to be inconvenienced. They ran out of coal and because most of there homes were heated by coalfires they soon felt very cold and miserable, and many of them blaimed the government for not giving a stronger lead. Coal was also still being used on the railways, and so many trains were late or were not running at all. The strike was also very impressionable because of its political importance.

c) The causes of the collapse of the general strike lay in the attitude of the government. The Prime Minister came on to radio and TV and said he could not allow the existence of the country to be threatened, and took steps to provide transport and food for the starving millions. The workers themselves, there funds depleted by many years of unemployment, could not stand the strain. The general feeling of the public was against there resort to undeclared industrial war. After a week, the trade unions admitted there defeat and had to go back to work, all but the miners, who straggled on all summer but finally had to accept the owner's terms. The general strike turned out to be very much of a 'nine day's wonder'.

Bibliography
English Economic History, Southgate
Modern British Economic History, Flynn
Modern Times, Macphail

2.2 Examiner's comments

This example is an object lesson in reading the question and keeping the answer strictly relevant to it. But the treatment of a) tends to be over-generalized, relating in an unfocused way to conditions in post-war Britain – a very useful *introduction* to the problems of the coal industry, but saying only a little about them in depth. The specific difficulties of the coal industry are not discussed, and the Sankey and Samuel Commissions, which could have shed some useful light on the problem, are omitted. The overall title of the assignment should have provided the student with a clue as to the best way of tackling it. Again, there are irritating spelling mistakes. There is also the assertion of a bland *non-reason*: 'The strike was widely supported because most of the workers were in favour of it' – which is a bit like saying 'Cromwell won the battle of Naseby because he didn't lose it'.

Answer (b) misses the point about the *General* Strike, and concentrates on the coal strike only, ignoring the parts played by the other unions at that time. It includes the error that there had not been a coal strike for a long time, when in fact there had been more than one since the

CHAPTER FIVE **RAILWAY BUILDING** 73

war. The answer begins with another truism: 'The strike made a great impression because it was important', and ends with another, almost precisely identical (though slightly less literate). What we should have had here is some consideration of the *impact* of the strike: the disappointments, frustration and irritation that brought it to a head; the combination of desperation and idealism that underlay it; and the sense of class solidarity that it produced – exhilarating the workers and frightening the authorities. No one on either side denied its importance; the government seeing the defeat of the strikers as its prime objective, and the workers attaching such significance to it that any defeat was bound to be represented as a betrayal. Long after the general strike as a political weapon had been exploded, it was still dreaded by the one and respected by the other.

In (c) perhaps the question was misread; if not misread, then it was ignored. What was needed was the effect of the collapse of the strike on labour history over the next twenty years. But what is offered are the immediate reasons *why* the strike was a failure – including the silly anachronism about TV! Better answers would have referred to the immediate repercussions: the enactment of the Trades Disputes Act of 1927; the divisions between the extremists and the moderates within the Conservative Party; the results for trade union membership and the finances of the Labour Party; and the reversal of fortunes in the election of 1929. Then it might have looked at the longer term results in the Depression of the 1930s – and even at the polls in the 1945 election! After 1926, the class war came to be fought within the framework of the constitution rather than outside it.

Though better than before, this work is of a fairly low standard and is in places quite off-target. Hence it would obtain only a low mark, despite the provision of a bibliography.

UNIT 3 RAILWAY BUILDING

▶ **Assessment objectives 3 and 4: Empathy and the use of sources**
Word limit 1,000 words.

Study the sources below, and then answer the question which follow.

Source A

Source B

Source C

Source D

Source E

Rude, rugged and uncultivated, possessed of great animal strength, collected in large numbers, living and working entirely together, they are a class and a community by themselves. Before the time when . . .inland navigation was called into existence, this class was unknown; but in these works the 'navigator' gained this title. The canal manias created the demand and increased the body; the great architectural works of the kingdom continued it; and when the rail began to spread its iron road through England, the labourer attracted no attention from politician or philosopher, from statistician or statesman; he had joined no important body, he had not made himself an object of dread. Rough alike in morals and manners, collected from the wild hills of Yorkshire and Lancashire, coming in troops from the fens of Lincolnshire, and afterwards an independent bearing; mostly dwelling apart from the villagers near whom they worked; with an untaught, undisciplined nature; impulsive and brute-like, regarded almost as outcasts, herding together like beasts of the field, with no moral law and no social ties, they increased with an increased demand, and from thousands grew to hundreds of thousands. They lived only for the present; they cared not for the past, and they were indifferent about the future.

(from J.R. Francis, *The History of the English Railway*, 1851.)

QUESTIONS

a) Study Sources A, B and C, and explain why it was necessary, in building the Victorian railways, to build *cuttings, tunnels* and *viaducts*.

b) What impression of Victorian engineering achievement is provided by these three sources? What are the most obvious differences between such scenes as they were in the nineteenth century, and as they would be at the present time?

c) Suggest reasons why the *navvies* portrayed in Source D look so neat and clean.

d) How well does the description given of the navvies in Source E match their appearnce in the photograph (Source D)?

e) How does Source E explain the name navvies, as applied in Source D, to these railway workers?

f) Source E tells us that the navvies *lived apart from the villagers near whom they worked*. How does the source explain this tendency not to mix?

g) Different inhabitants of the village – the school mistress, the vicar, the publican, the village girls, the shop-keeper – had greatly different attitudes towards the navvies in the district. What were these attitudes, and how do you account for them?

3.1 A student's answer

a) The gradients on Victorian railway lines were strictly limited. With locomotives lighter than they are today it was impossible for an engine to keep its grip on the track if the slope was too stepp, especially if it was hauling a heavy load of freight or passengers. Hence cuttings were made through hills in order to avoid the line having to climb and then to descend again, whilst tunnels were excavated if it was not practicable to have a cutting. Viaducts were necessary to carry railways lines across rivers or through marshy ground, and were also used as a convenient route from one side to the other of a steep-sided valley.

b) The main impression given by these photographs is of the immense energy and discipline of the manual worker in Victorian times. The level of technology he employed may look rather crude to the modern eye, but his efforts were well-directed and controlled and the engineering that went into the building of railways was detailed and accurate. The bridges and tunnels were built to last, and many of them are still in use today.

The obvious difference evident from these scenes relates to the conspicuous lack of heavy construction machinery. These workers seem to have done everything by hand. They use wheelbarrows and picks and shovels; they shore up rock and earth with wooden planking laborioulsy installed by hand. There is no pre-stressed concrete; they build their walls and piers laboriously, cementing stone to stone. There are no bulldozers, no dragline scrapers, no big earth-moving lorries. Horses are used and there are some steam-driven machines, but there is nothing driven by petrol or by diesel.

c) They normally were much dirtier and more untidy than they seem to be here; they had presumably smartened themselves up for the photograph they knew was about to be taken.

d) Not very well. In the photograph they are shown as orderly and rather respectable, with little sign of their being 'undisciplined' or 'impulsive and brute-like.' We have to remember, however, that they were on their best behaviour in posing for the photograph, and this does not give entirely a reliable impression. If their faces are more closely examined, indeed, they can be seen to have the appearance of rather rough and uneducated men.

e) Source E explains the term 'navvy' by giving its original usage. The labourers who first dug the canals in the early nineteenth century were known as 'navigators' because of their association with what were often called 'inland navigations', though these men did not actually navigate at all. Later the term was shortened to 'navvy' and came to be used for railway builders as well as canal builders.

f) Navvies did not mix much with the villagers near whose homes they worked because, according to Source E, they were 'impulsive and brute-like' and had 'untaught, undisciplined natures', so that they were regarded 'almost as outcasts.' They were said to be 'like beasts of the field', without 'moral laws' or 'social ties.' They 'lived only for the present' and did not care about the future.

g) Different inhabitants of the village regarded the navvies differently. The school mistress was probably appalled by their ignorance and personally rather frightened of them, but reactions were by no means predictable. Some village girls liked to hang around with them and helped them spend their money, though others would not want to let themselves fall into the hands of such rough and unpredictable men. Fellow workers might keep away from them, thinking them a violent, unpredictable lot; but others might be a little envious of them with their nomadic life and their handsome wages. Some publicans and shop-keepers welcomed the money they spent in their establishments, but would soon protest against the rougher side of their nature if they quarrelled and began to smash up the place. Some churchmen would regard them with mistrust and dread, hoping they would keep well away, but others would take the view that they were human beings with souls and they should do their best to understand them. The village children might cower in corners and hide from them, yet many had families of their own and could show themselves quite capable of tenderness in dealing with children, so that their initial fears might later be overcome. As far as working men went, navvies were relatively well-paid at this time, and this alone provided them with a certain amount of status in the village. Nor were all of them rough and uncouth. A numer of work-gangs were equipped with portable homes built out of wood which they moved with them from place to place, with it was not unusual for these roving settlements to have a portable church too, which could be put up and taken down as required. If they were Irish Catholics they would naturally attend service there. Others, even if they were not churchgoers, might well be decent enough fellows at heart.
(*906 words.*)

3.2 Examiner's comments

The treatment of a) and b) is pithy and discerning. In c) it could be argued that this occasion was something other than a working day; the men appeared to be dressed in their best clothes, or they have come in clean clothes to have the photograph taken before changing for work. The statement in d) that their faces show that they were rough and uneducated seems too bold an effort at stereotyping. It is certainly difficult to substantiate on this evidence – by their appearance some of these men could even be respectable schoolmasters!

The explanation in e) is clear and accurate, whilst the answer to f) makes it quite clear why the navvies were not considered to be the sort of people fit to mix with village society. This sub-answer is also one which makes extensive – but not uncritical – use of the source in the form of selected quotations. The final sub-question is tackled with good empathy.

The assignment as a whole would earn a high grade, or even a top one.

CHAPTER FIVE EXAMPLES OF STUDENTS' COURSEWORK

UNIT 4: WOMEN IN SOCIETY, 1890–1940

▸ Assessment objectives 3 and 4: Empathy and the use of sources
Word Limit: 1000 words.

Study the sources below, and then answer the questions which follow.

Source A

A really sensible girl will not spend much money on her trousseau, though I have heard it said that . . . a girl who has no dowry should furnish her wardrobe plentifully, especially with underclothes.

Already possessing a few clothes for her back, she actually requires for her trousseau: 3 nightdresses, silk, cotton or woollen as desired; 4 to 6 shifts or combinations; 8 pairs of stockings – 3 woollen, 3 black silk or Lisle thread, and a couple of pairs of white silk or lace for evening wear; 2 corsets; 2 summer vests, 4 winter; 3 white petticoats – 2 good and one handsome; 2 evening bodices or slips; and 2 coloured woollen, or 6 linen bodies; 6 pairs of boots and shoes for bad weather and day wear, and evening and fireside slippers; one dressing gown; one toilet jacket of flannel; 12 collars, or a few yards of frilling; 12 towels; at least 2 dozen handkerchiefs – plenty will be wanted, not only for colds in the head, but even, perhaps, who knows? for tears; cuffs and gloves as required; and last, but not least, nice handsome travelling trunks, and a well-fitted dressing-bag to pack them all in.

(Mrs Haweis, *The Art of Housekeeping*, 1889.)

Source B

There is scarcely a lower class of girls to be found than the girls of the Woolwich 'Dusthole'. The women living and following their dreadful business in this neighbourhood are so degraded that even abandoned men will refuse to accompany them home. Soldiers are forbidden to enter the place, or to go down the street, on pain of twenty-five days imprisonment; pickets are stationed at either end to prevent this.

One public house is shut up three or four times a day sometimes for fear of losing the licence through the terrible brawls which take place within. A policeman never goes down this street alone at night – one having died not long ago from injuries received there – but our two Salvation Army lasses go unharmed and loved at all hours, spending every other night upon the streets.

The girls sink to the Dusthole after coming down several grades. There is but one on record who came there with beautiful clothes, and this poor girl, when last seen by the officers, was a pauper in the workhouse infirmary in a wretched condition.

The lowest class of all is the girls who stand at the pier-head – these sell themselves literally for a bare crust of bread and sleep in the streets.

(William Booth, *In Darkest England, and the Way Out*, 1890.)

Fig 5.18
A socialite arriving, before 1914, to see the horse show at Olympia

Fig 5.19
Two girls painting the girders of a railway station in the early days of the First World War

Source C

Source D

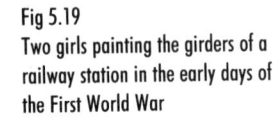

Fig 5.20
Landgirls harvesting flax in 1916

Source E

Source F

Ann Veronica (1909) was a youthful heroine who was allowed a frankness of desire and sexual enterprise hitherto unknown in English popular fiction. That book created a scandal at the time, though it seems mild enough reading to the youth of today . . . The particular offence was that Ann Veronica was a virgin who fell in love and showed it, instead of waiting as all popular heroines had hitherto done, for someone to make love to her. It was held to be an unspeakable offence that an adolescent female should be sex-conscious before the thing was forced upon her attention. But Ann Veronica wanted a particular man who excited her and she pursued him and got him . . .

It was a strenuous and long-sustained fuss. The book was banned by libraries and preached against by earnest clergymen. The spirit of denunciation was aroused and let loose against me.

(H.G. Wells *An Experiment in Autobiography*, 1934.)

QUESTIONS

a) Study Source A. What do you understand by the word *trousseau*, and why was this example said to be useful for a *really sensible girl*?
b) What do Sources A and B tell us of the differing fortunes of young women in Victorian times?
c) 'Social butterflies.' How appropriate, according to Source C, especially for the women, was this description of upper-class behaviour before the First World War?
d) What different types of dress and behaviour for women, according to Sources D and E, became appropriate during the course of the First World War? What helps to explain this change in public attitudes?
e) Why should the subject-matter of the book *Ann Veronica*, as referred to in Source F, have seemed so offensive to many contemporaries at the time it was published? How far was this repugnance beginning to break up twenty years later?
f) How would a student of women's history use *all* these sources to show that underlying attitudes towards women did not change very much during the period under examination?
g) What arguments would have been used by women in the 1930s in favour of, and against, women's emancipation?

4.1 A student's answer

a) 'Trousseau' is a French word meaning 'bundle', and is used to describe the collection of things going towards a bride's outfit. It usually refers to her clothing, but sometimes is used more widely to include household goods like pillow-cases and table-cloths.

Presumably the authoress means that it would be sensible for a girl to ensure that she was well provided for before getting married, so that she would not have to keep asking her husband for money to buy things when they were newly-wed. The idea, too, if she had no dowry, would be that to go into marriage well provided for would to a small extent compensate her husband financially for the lack of a settlement.

b) The girl for whom the authoress is writing in Source A seems to be quite well-off to be able to buy for herself the huge heap of things that are recommended. Some of the items, such as silk stockings 'for evening wear' and 'good' or 'handsome' petticoats also suggest a middle-class setting for the girl to live in. A working-class girl would have neither the quality nor the quantity of this kind of clothing.

The girls described by William Booth are clearly of the lowest class, living in rags and filth, surrounded by rowdy drunks and earning their meagre living by the vilest form of prostitution. Only the girls at the pier-head, waiting to sell themselves to sailors as they disembark, are worse. The area where they live is so violent and sordid that even soldiers and policemen are well-advised to keep away.

The two sources together show the enormous inequalities of Victorian England.

c) The young woman in Photograph C certainly has the appearance of a butterfly; she is pretty, elegantly dressed in a beautiful dress with masses of petticoats, and wearing a hat with flowers on it. She is being courteously handed down from a taxi by a man who is presumably her beau.

The phrase 'social butterfly', however, implies a kind of decorative uselessness and suggests perhaps that she is one of the idle rich. This may be true or not; there is not enough evidence here to be able to be sure of it. At the same time, it is clear that for her to be dressed as beautifully as this, and to have the time and the inclination to attend the horse show, she is already a member of the leisured classes, or aspiring to join them by marrying her young man.

d) During the First World War women began to do jobs that had previously been the preserve of men. They drove buses and trams, delivered letters and even worked in munitions factories. The girls in Sources D and E are seen doing necessary maintenance jobs high up in the girders of a railway station, and working in the fields as land-girls, getting in the harvest. Women had always done manual labour in many sectors of the economy such as textile mills, but the trade unions had only just agreed to the 'dilution' of labour by letting women do more jobs.

Women doing this kind of work began to wear trousers commonly for the first time, and to keep their hair pinned up under close-fitting caps. This was partly in the interests of safety, to prevent the hair getting entangled in moving machinery, and partly for the sake of ease and convenience, since no one can clamber round girders doing a paint job if they are encumbered in skirts and petticoats.

It would have been considered rather shocking for women to dress and to behave in public in this way before the war, though some of them must have done already (some of them smoked pipes, for that matter). These things would have obviously conflicted with the accepted image of women. But the war brought a relaxation of standards, and women began to drink in public houses and even smoke in public.

e) Older people might have been shocked by the extract quoted because it was stated so directly. It contained strong language, like 'sexual enterprise', 'virgin' and 'sex-conscious', and it also expressed very frankly the idea that women ought to be just as free to chase men as men to chase women. There was always a bit of the naughty boy in H.G. Wells, and no doubt he enjoyed shocking his contemporaries.

By 1934 this attitude was beginning to change, though even then women who pursued men were often still denounced as 'forward hussies'. Perhaps men found it damaging to their egos that they were not entirely accepted as dominant, picking amongst their female playthings. It is interesting that, according to Wells, the clergy were amongst those who wished to see the traditional male dominance maintained.

f) All the sources show a flavouring of the traditional attitudes towards women. A speaks with a certain archness of handkerchiefs wanted 'not only for colds in the head, but even, perhaps, who knows?, for tears,' B speaks of Salvation Army 'lasses' with condescending familiarity and goes on to say how much they were 'loved'. Source C is perhaps most direct in reinforcing the stereotype of Edwardian courtesy. D and E were photographed because of their novelty, and in the former the workers are being eyed by passers-by below with some curiosity. In Source F, Wells recalls the 'strenuous and long-sustained fuss' from traditionalists that greeted his frank treatment of female sexuality in Anne Veronica in 1909, and his comments on female stereotyping were not entirely inappropriate in 1934.

g) Those favouring women's emancipation would take the view that women had been subjected to male domination for too long, and that modern conditions made their continued subjection unnecessary and harmful. This century had seen some improvement but further progress was long overdue. Too many occupations were closed to women, and women's inclination to live their own lives was frustrated in too many trivial ways. Society permitted harrassment, voyeurism and discrimination on the part of male- dominated society ,and females were often lacking in economic muscle in business and exploited in the home. They were neglected as an area of academic study and their champions were frequently regarded as cranks.

Those against further emancipation would argue that equality could not be legislated, and if women were to obtain it they would have to desert it. Many women might not wish to forfeit the image of themselves as the gentler sex, and might be quite content to choose a domestic role in spite of the strident campaigning of their feminist sisters. They would argue that there were now relatively few occupations closed to women, and there were good reasons for closing those that were. Unionization and equal pay were acceptable for many women, but not for those who did not regard career work as their prime objective, but chose to work as part-timers or for sums less than the established rate. Some of the feminist proposals might have the unwelcome effect of making the situation of women worse, instead of better. (1156 words.)

4.2 Examiner's comments

This is an excellent piece of work throughout, with an insight and a degree of perception unusual in GCSE. The balanced judgement in c) and the argument in f) are particularly to be commended as models of their kind. 'Voyeurism' in g) is an adult concept which shows the maturity of this candidate's thought. This is undoubtedly a Grade A answer.

UNIT 5 WAR AND SOCIAL AND ECONOMIC CHANGE

▶ Assessment objective 2: Cause and consequence
Word limit: 600 words

QUESTION

'War is a great accelerator of social and economic change.' Referring to any one war of which you have knowledge, show how far you agree with this statement.

5.1 Student's answer: Version 1

The immediate effect of the outbreak of war in 1914 was that thousands of men volunteered for service in the armed forces in Britain. Many of them served in other countries during the war, such as France, Belgium, Italy, the Balkans and the Middle East and in the colonies. Conscription, introduced in 1916, increased the flow of men into the services even more rapidly, so that by the end of the war there were nearly four million men under arms. Their departure left a serious shortage of labour. Into the gap stepped women. In July 1915 there was a great women's War Pageant, when thousands of women marched through London and sent a deputation to meet the Minister for Munitions, Lloyd George. To him they pledged their assistance in the struggle. Soon valuable and dangerous work was being done by women munitions workers. They filled the shells and made the bullets. They worked long hours; twelve hours daily was not unusual. Many were killed in factory explosions.

But the men in the army had an even tougher time. In the horror of the trenches on the Western Front and on the beaches of Gallipoli thousands went to their deaths in the grimmest war the world had ever seen. The use of poison gas and the frightful new scientific weapons caused terrible casualties, and though our men had the tank the surprise effect of this was lost and it did not decide the war as quickly as its inventors thought. Before Armistice Day, many thousands had lain down their lives for their country in endless slaughter on the Somme and at Passchendaele. Cavalry was not used so much in their war as previously. Men and materials were now transported by motor lorries, and horses played a smaller part. Other animals, however, played important parts in the war. Dogs were used for carrying messages, and sometimes Red Cross dogs were employed to seek out wounded men on the battlefield. Pigeons were pressed into service in large numbers, and the armies had their lofts behind the lines. Thousands of reports and other messages were carried by the birds, some of them of vital importance. One French pigeon was even awarded the Legion of Honour for its flights through the storms of fire at the siege of Verdun in 1916. Medical services were also improved and thousands of women gave their help and encouragement in the VAD. Many 'Tommies', if not killed outright, 'got a Blighty one' and came back to Britain on sick leave before being invalided out of the services.

During the war there were many new inventions and the march of progress continued. Washing machines, with a handle at the top to circulate the clothes in the tub came into use. The zip fastener was an important invention in 1914, and the brassiere was invented for women. Traffic lights were also invented at this time, though they did not appear on the streets of London until after 1918. But generally supplies of goods were short, and there was considerable inflation. Women and often children spent hours in shopping queues waiting for meagre supplies of meat, sugar and even things such as potatoes. Before the end of the war, rationing was introduced by Lord Rhondda but the effort was enormous and the scheme so complicated that it wore him out and he died. There was however much less drunkenness than before the war and the civilian morale remained good throughout. This was in spite of the blackout which had to be introduced when Zeppelins started raiding southern towns and cities.

Britain and other European powers also borrowed heavily during the war from countries such as the USA, and these debts, together with the punishing losses of shipping during the U-Boat campaign, made Britain's post-war recovery very difficult. At the end of the war many people had a quite different outlook, and short skirts and prohibition in the 1920s were an indication of these changes. European powers also had to make repayments of what they had borrowed out of German reparations, so that at the end of the war they were not really any better off.

Generally, however, the end of the war was a time of great optimism. Returning soldiers hoped that they would, find what the Prime Minister called 'homes fit for heroes to live in', for there was now a greater awareness that social problems had to be dealt with if the country was to avoid revolution. Schools were different, too. During the war the school-leaving age had ben put up to 14, and there were 'continuation' schools for pupils who were older than that. There was also an improvement in the standard of living of British citizens.
(784 words.)

Bibliography
S.R. Gibbons & P. Morican, World War One, Longman Modern Times, 1965.
D, Lindsay & E.S. Washington, Britain Between the Exhibitions, 1851–1951, OUP, 1960.
Eureka! Sunday Times Magazine History of Inventions, 1970.
Jack Watson, British History Since 1914, Murray, 1983.

Now compare Version 1 with Version 2 below. Remember to check again exactly what it is that the student is supposed to be answering.

5.2 Student's answer: Version 2

Economic progress in Britain was already begining to slow down before 1914, with dimminishing industrial productivity and a high level of unemployment accept in the armaments industrys. In many ways the Edwardian period was an 'Indian summer' of British grateness. Markets were being lost to our competitors overseas, and though Britian was still investing heavily in forreign countrys, much of the investment was meerly reeinvestment of earlier profits.

The war administered a sharp shock to the British ecconomy. Many of the cosy arrangements between manufacturers were broken down as production stepped up, and Lloyd George worked very hard as Minister of Munitions to supply the armies overseas with as many guns and shells as they needed. Trade unions were perswaded to abandon strikes and other restrictive practises, and to accept women workers into their ranks. Short-time working seized in the mines and on the railways, and the whole country made a tremendous war effort, especially in steel and munitions. The farmers, too, gave all they had for the war effort, and the country did its best to become self-sufficient. The level of taxes rose sharply, as did consumer prices, but moral remained high and the country reached new levels of productive efficiensy.

But not all the trends which were accelerated by the war were favourable ones. The war brought a serioous loss of overseas markets, and British losses of shipping, meant a decline in our league position as the world's leading carrier. Other countrys fostered the growth of their home industrys, and this in turn brought fewer overseas outlets for British goods. We also continued to heavily import foodstuffs and raw materials, though we were not in a position to pay for them, and as a result we had to liquidate many of our overseas investments, built up over a century. The pound sterlings was also weaker than it had been before the war, because in the course of the war we were forced to suspend the gold standard which was also inflationary.

The process of social change was also speeded up. The coalition government extended the boundaries of the state and regulated many features of life preeviously left to chance e.g. social control if not ownership of the coal mines, and regulation of wages and bread prices. The Civil Service grew and there was a host of new government ministries. Drunkenness and crime amongst the working classes declined sharply. The emancipation of women continued more rapidly, and socially women began to mix more readily. They took up jobs previously reerved for men, and began to smoke and go into pubs. In 1918 many of them got the vote. A high level of earnings during the war, and the farer sharing of war burdens such as brought about by rationing meant less social
inequality. Even children had a better deal after the Fisher Education Act of 1918. There was a new air of optimism at the end of the war, and the working classes had achieved a new independance and dignity.
(499 words.)

5.3 Examiner's comments

At first glance you may well think the first answer is better than the second: it is a good deal longer. It has a short, but well-presented bibliography, and it is certainly better spelt. But if you look more closely you will see that whilst the first version has a lot of material, much of it is descriptive – it does not seem to be geared to the acceleration of economic and social change. There is a link established at some length between service in the armed forces leading to the employment of women but the idea of change does not come across so clearly as it does with less material in Version 2. The reference to factory explosions needs qualification: there were several major accidents, including one very costly of life in 1916, but factory disasters were not, in general, a major hazard. The lengthy second paragraph of Version 1 describes the horrors of war, but not of economic and social change, and the reference to a short and rather odd list of inventions which follows does not show the war as an accelerator of this change. The answer continues on a descriptive path and ends with references to war debts and social problems which are true and could be made to be relevant but which in fact are not very analytically handled.

Version 2, on the other hand, attempts to tackle the question set. Certainly the various changes are linked to the war, and the accelerating effect of the war is implied or stated. Its material is rather thin and the whole answer could have done with a little more development, together with a summing up of 'how far' the war accelerated the changes. (It could be argued that in many areas, particularly social, the change was limited.) It seems a pity, too, that the candidate does not see fit to provide a bibliography; the examiner would have appreciated seeing what sources the candidate had consulted. But at least the second version is mainly analytical while the first is largely descriptive and gives the impression of being rather random – even miscellaneous – in construction. Version 1 touches on some of the main themes without exploring them and was awarded a middling grade; Version 2 is much more effectively on target, and was awarded a high grade.

CHAPTER FIVE EXAMPLES OF STUDENTS' COURSEWORK

UNIT 6 NINETEENTH-CENTURY RAILWAYS

▸ **Assessment objectives 3 and 4: Empathy, and the use of sources**
Word limit: 600 words
Study the sources below, and then answer the questions which follow:

Source A

We were introduced to the little engine which was to drag us along the rails. She – for they make these curious little fire-horses all mares – consisted of a boiler, a stove, a small platform, a bench, and behind the bench a barrel containing enough water to prevent her being thirsty for fifteen miles . . . She goes upon two wheels, which are her feet, and are moved by bright steel legs called pistons; these are propelled by steam . . . This snorting little animal, which I felt rather inclined to pat, was harnessed to our carriage, and Mr Stephenson having taken me on the bench of the engine with him, we started at about ten miles an hour . . . You can't imagine how strange it seemed to be journeying on thus, without any visible cause of progress other than the magical machine, with its flying white breath and rythmical, unvarying pace, between rocky walls. Bridges are thrown from side to side across the top of these cliffs, and the people looking down upon us from them seemed like pygmies standing in the sky.
(Description by Fanny Kemble, 1830, of a journey on the Liverpool-Manchester Rly.)

Source B

There is now no hazard, as there was then, of being informed that there is 'no room' – there are no unreasonable demands from extortionate guards to satisfy, no clambering over dirty wheels, no hurting one's shins on sharp irons, no wedging of oneself amidst piles of luggage on a lofty unsheltered platform, around which numerous legs hang dangling; while, if it rains, it is not necessary for one's own comfort that the drip of our umbrella should be turned into a neighbour's neck. And at the same time a pleasant thought to many that while the train bowls over the iron road, there is no plying of the whip, no foaming mouths; but that the great power which thus swiftly bears us onwards has bones of brass and iron, and nerves and muscles that cannot tire.
(A description by Edward Pease, Quaker industrialist, comparing rail travel with the stage coach about 1845.)

Source C

Does anybody mean to say that decent people, passengers, would consent to be hurried through the air upon a railroad . . . or is it to be imagined that women would endure the fatigue, the misery and danger of being dragged at the rate of twenty miles an hour, all their lives being at the mercy of a tin pipe, a copper boiler, or the accidental dropping of a pebble on the line of way?
(Col. Charles Sibthorpe, MP, about 1830, on railway travel.)

Source D

Nothing is more distasteful to me than to hear the echo of our hills reverberating with the noise of hissing railraod engines, running through the heart of our hunting country, and destroying the noble sport I have been accustomed to from my childhood.
(George Fitzhardinge Berkeley, landowner about 1830 on railway building.)

Source E

> Is then no nook of English ground secure
> From rash assault? Schemes of retirement sown
> In youth, and 'mid the busy world kept pure
> And when their earliest flowers of hope were blown,
> Must perish – how can they this blight endure?

(William Wordsworth, on the proposed extension of the Kendal and Windermere Rly., about 1845.)

Source F

When a passenger arrives at the terminus at the busiest time in August he is immediately separated from his luggage, in a way which would do honour to the new Poor Law. He then enters into a waiting room, which has the appearance of never having been acquainted with the use of soap and water, from the lower end of which no very agreeable odour arises; upon the signal from a diminutive bell, the barriers are removed and two or three hundred passengers rush pell-mell up the grand staircase . . . A scene of confusion now arises from the carriages of the up-train not being yet empty; into these pens the greatest possible number of passengers are crowded, with the least possible regard to their comfort.
(Description of the London-Blackwall Rly., from the *Railway Times*, 1844.)

CHAPTER FIVE NINETEENTH-CENTURY RAILWAYS 83

Source G

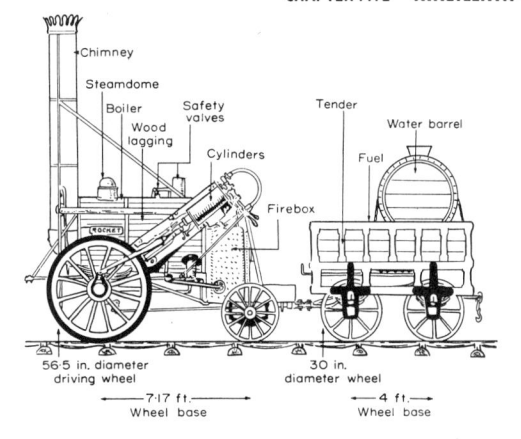

Fig 5.1
The Rocket

QUESTIONS

a) What impression of travel on the early railways is given by the writer of Source A? Why did she say that she 'felt rather inclined to pat' the steam engine?
b) How far is the description given by the author of Source A in agreement with the drawing given in Source G?
c) What kind of preference is expressed by the author of Source B between coach and rail travel, and for what reasons?
d) Which of the authors in sources A to F favour the railways, and which oppose them? Quote words and phrases from the sources to justify your answer.
e) Select *three* of the sources which express opposition to the idea of railways, and explain in each case the interests they thought they were trying to defend.
f) To what social class would you say the authors of the sources belonged? Why is working-class opinion so under-represented in this selection? What different opinions about railways would have been put forward by working-class people if they had been asked?

6.1 A student's answer

a) The impression given by the writer is that everything was on a small scale. She refers to the 'little engine', and her describtion gives the impression that there was a platform and a bench and the driver was sitting in the open air. The describtion is also a bit twee, with the author saying that she would have liked to pat this little animal. When she says she would have liked to pat it, she seems to be pretending that it is really a kind of mechanical horse. She says it is a 'snorting little animal' with feet and legs, and she does not want it to be thirsty for fifteen miles. All the same, the journey must have been very slow, if it was only at a speed of 'ten miles an hour' as she says. It would also have been very informal, for the writer seems to have traveled for at least part of the way on the locomotive with 'Mr Stephenson.'

b) The engine does not look much like a 'little fire-horse', but it is certainly true that it consisted of the things which the author of Source A listed – 'a boiler, a stove, a small platform, a bench and behind the bench, a barrel.' From the describtion and the illustration, it looks as though Fanny Kemble may have actually traveled on the Rocket.

c) The author of Source B preffers to travel by rail instead of by coach. He says this is because they are less crowded, and there are not so many demands for tips from railway staff as there were from the gaurds who worked for the coaching companies. He also says it is cleaner, and that people are less likely to injure themselves clambering aboard a train than climbing on top of a coach. He gives the impression that it was very uncomfortable traveling on top of a coach, especially if it rained, because then the rain trickled down your neck from the edge of the umbrella of the man sitting next to you. The notion that trains belching out dirt and fumes and sprinkling every traveller with soot and sparks were cleaner than coaches seems to the modern reader a bit unlikely, but perhaps for this author the novelty hadn't yet worn off.

d) Fanny Kemble is rather taken with railway engines and seems to like them. She says that the locomotive is like 'a snorting little animal which I rather felt inclined to pat.' Edward Peas also seems to favour railways and seems to think they are safer. He says 'There is now no hazzard.' Col. Charles Sibthorpe does not like them at all, and suggests that women will be frightened by them. He also says they are not safe, and asks who would wish to be 'at the mercy of a tin pipe' or 'a copper boiler'? George Berkeley also hates the railways because he doesn't want to see his hunting spoiled, saying; 'nothing is more distasteful' than the railways. Wordsworth is a poetical old buffer who seems to have lost his sense of humour and calls the advance of the railways 'a rash assault' on the countreyside. In Source F the author tells us of the trials of having to put up with dirty, crowded railway stations, with people rushing to get on the trains. He says 'two or three hundred passengers rush pell-mell up the grand staircase.' He also complains about losing his luggage.

e) The three I choose are: C, D and E. In C, the author thought he was defending decency and the modesty of women. Like many MPs the opposed any change as though it was unheard of, and produced a lot of conventional excuses for keeping things as they were, showing the same unlikely concern for the ladies as present- day members do for old-age pensioners. In D, the author seems to think he is defending the environment against the hisses and the whistles of the railway engines. He does not say here that railway engines would frighten the farm animals, but this is probably what he thinks. In Source E, the poet expresses concern for the elderly, pointing out that old people who want to retire to a caravan in the Lake District will be inconvenienced by the coming of the railways. He sees the railways as a 'blight' on the countreyside in this very scenic area.

f) All the authors sound very middle-class. Fanny Kemble was a famous actress, and would have been accepted in high social circles. Peas was an industrialist, Sibthorpe an MP and Berkeley a landowner. By the 1840s Wordsworth had become an establishment figure, however outragious his opinions had been in his youth. We cannot be sure who the writer in Source F is, but the fact that he wrote for a journal suggests he was one of the scribbling classes.

Working-class people would not have left any records at that time, since all of them were ilitterate. But if they had, we should find that they had widely differentiated empathies about the railways. Many would not have been able to afford to travel on them, and would continue to walk everywhere; they would have thought that railways were an uneccessary luxury. They might also have felt rather snobish towards the upper-class people who used them. Others would have thought they were a good idea. This was because the railways created work for the lower orders, and some towns like Swindon and Crewe grew up specially to cater for railways. So they would have welcomed them, even if they could not afford to travel on them themselves.
(894 words.)

6.2 Examiner's comments

This set of answers, with its unreliable spelling, is rather mixed in quality. The text of a) offers more than 'small scale' and 'slow' speed as impressions of travel, and words like 'twee' should be avoided. The idea of 'patting' the mechanical horse is well captured, though the reasons for her saying so could have been brought out. The candidate, though brief, is on target in b) – but the diagram shows more than two wheels (a *two-wheeled* engine would have been rather unstable!). Part c) is quite well done, and the final comment on the novelty justified; perhaps Pease's comments would have been better understood if the candidate had realized his close connection with iron production and the huge demand for iron brought about by the growth of the railways. The supporters and opponents of railways are in general accurately represented in d), though it is not quite acceptable to describe Wordsworth as 'a poetical old buffer.' The interests in e) are not well brought out: Sibthorpe's opposition is probably that of a landowner using the women's angle as a better defence against railways than the naked self-interest of the landowning class; Berkeley is defending hunting rather than farm animals in general; and Wordsworth would have been horrified to see the Lake District disfigured with caravans. The candidate starts off on the right track in f), but suggestions that *all* the working class were illiterate undermine his credibility – and 'differentiated empathies' strikes an odd note and sounds like an attempt at mark-grabbing. The use of the term the 'scribbling classes', with its echoes of contemporary journalism, strikes the same note of frivolity as did the word 'twee' earlier, and makes the examiner think that the candidate is not entirely serious in this answer. More substantially, the point could have been made that, especially after the Act of 1844, but in many cases before it, the railways offered the possibility of cheap travel previously unavailable to the working classes, and brought countryside and seaside within reach of those who wished to escape, if only for a few hours, the squalor of early Victorian towns.

There is intelligent reading of the documents here, and a good deal of useful analysis in the answers overall, and it would have secured a good average mark.

UNIT 7 CHILD LABOUR IN THE NINETEENTH CENTURY

▶ **Assessement objective 4: Use of sources**
Word limit: 600 words.

Study the sources below, and then answer the questions which follow:

Source A

We find that instances occur in which children are taken into these mines to work as early as four years of age, sometimes at five, and between five and six, not infrequently between six and seven, and often from seven to eight; whilst from eight to nine is the ordinary age at which employment in the mines commences.

(from the 1842 Report of the Children's Employment Commission (Mines))

Source B

I'm a trapper in Gawber pit. I have to trap without light and I'm scared. I go at four and sometimes half-past three in the morning, and come out at five and half-past; I never got to sleep. Sometimes I sing when I've light, but not in the dark; I daren't sing then. I don't like being in the pit.

(Evidence of Sarah Goodyer, 8 years old, in the 1842 Report)

Source C

The girl has first to descend a nine-ladder pit to the first rest . . . to draw up the baskets or tubs of coals filled by the bearers; she then takes her creel (a basket formed to the back, not unlike a cockle-shell, flattened towards the neck and shoulders) and pursues her journey to the wall-face . . . She then lays down her basket, into which the coal is rolled, and it is frequently more than one man can do to lift the burden on her back. The straps are then placed over the forehead . . . The height ascended, and the distance along the roads, added together, exceed the height of St Paul's Cathedral; and it not infrequently happens that the straps break, and the load falls upon those females who are following.

(from the 1842 Report of the Children's Employment Commission (Mines))

Source D

I worked at Mr Swaine's at Little Gomersall, near Leeds. I earned half-a-crown a week from six to half-past seven. I came as a spinner . . . Mr Swaine's was a bad factory for cruelty to children in my time; I have marks on me now from ill-treatment that I got there. They would strike us with the billy-roller over the head. I have a bump on my head now from that.

(from the Report of the Committee on Factory Children's Labour, 1832)

Source E

Question: The common hours of labour were from six in the morning to half-past eight at night?
Answer: Yes.
Question: Were the children excessively fatigued by this labour?
Answer: Many times; we have cried often when we have given them the little victualling we had to give them. We had to shake them, and they have fallen asleep with the victuals in their mouths many a time.
Question: Have any of them had any accident in consequence of this labour?
Answer: Yes, my eldest daughter when she first went there . . . the cog caught her forefinger nail and screwed it off below the knuckle, and she was five weeks in Leeds Infirmary.

(from the Report of the Committee on Factory Children's Labour, 1832)

Source F

The owner told me that nothing could be so useful to a country as factories. 'You see these children, sir,' said he. 'In most parts of England poor children are a burden to parents and to poor rates; here the parish is freed from that expense. The children can earn their bread from the time they can walk. They come at five in the morning and leave at seven in the evening and another lot take over for the night; the wheels never stand still.'

(Robert Southey, *Espriella's Letters from England* 1811)

Source G

As to the conclusion I have come to from the working of my mill for 11 instead of 12 hours each day, I am quite satisfied that both as much yarn and cloth may be produced at quite as low a cost in 11 as in 12 hours. It is my intention to make a further reduction to 10½ hours, without the slightest fear of loss. I find the hands work with greater energy and spirit; they are more cheerful and happy.

(A factory owner quoted in *Parliamentary Papers*, 1845)

Source H

We have been told that our navy was the glory of the country, and that our maritime commerce and manufactures were the mainstay of the realm. We have also been told that the land had its share in our greatness, and should justly be considered as the pride and glory of England. The Bank, also, has put in its claim to share in this praise, and has stated that public credit is due to it; but now a most surprising discovery has been made, namely, that all our greatness and prosperity, that our superiority over other nations, is owing to 300,000 little girls in Lancashire.
(A speech in Parliament by William Cobbett, quoted by John Fielden in *The Curse of the Factory System*, 1836)

Source J

Fig 5.2
How children were sent down to the coal face, cross-lapped on a clatch iron, about 1840 (contemporary engraving)

Source K

Fig 5.3
A trapper opening a ventilation door for two children 'hurrying' a tub of coal, about 1840 (contemporary engraving)

Source L

Fig 5.4
Children in a British cotton mill, about 1840 (contemporary engraving)

CHAPTER FIVE CHILD LABOUR IN THE NINETEENTH CENTURY

QUESTIONS

a) Identify in each of Sources A-E one way in which conditions of children's labour was greatly different from today. What impression overall do these sources give of child labour in the nineteenth century?

b) How do the views of factory employers as quoted in Sources F and G resemble, and how far do they differ, from each other?

c) Besides the labour of factory children, what else did the speaker in Source H regard as the main causes of Britain's greatness in the early nineteenth century? How does the tone of this source differ from the tone of Sources A-G?

d) To what dangers, according to Sources J, K and L, were working children exposed at this time?

e) How far do Sources J, K and L bear out the evidence given in Sources A-E?

f) How reliable, in your opinion, are Sources F, G and H? How does their reliability compare with that of Sources A-E?

g) What types of sources, other than the types used here, would a historian wish to use in order to research more fully the question of juvenile employment in the early nineteenth century?

7.1 A student's answer

a) In Source A, the children start work very young. In B they work in the dark and are not allowed to sleep. In C, they are doing heavy manual labour hawling coal. In D, they are subject to physical abuse by their employers. In E, they are the victims of grewsome accidents. All the sauces show that conditions of work for young people were very bad.

b) Source F and G are similar because they both think that child labour is a good thing, because the 'wheels have to be kept turning.' They differ because the first one thinks that child labour keeps people off the Poor Rate, whilst the second doesn't mention this.

c) Manufacture, commerce and the Bank of England. This source differs in tone because it is written in vague and bombastic language by a member of Parliament who probably knew nothing about it. For him to claim that Britain's prosperity depended on the labour of '300,000 little girls' seems very harsh and unfeeling, as well as being quite untrue.

d) When children were being wound down the mine sitting 'cross-lapped' on an iron bar, there was always the danger, according to Source J, that they would fall down the shaft. The trapper in Source K was also exposed to danger, especially when he was working in the dark. He might get run over by a coal waggon, or crushed against the ventilation door. The children in Source L do not seem to be exposed to danger, except the one who is underneath the loom. He might easily get caught in the moving machinery and get injured.

e) Source J is similar to C, both being about going down the mine, one by ladder, the other going down a shaft on a rope. K is very much like B, both being about children acting as ventilation trappers. Source L is about conditions in textile mills and is like E, which mentions children getting injured by machinery.

f) Sauces F, G and H are not very reliable because they are biased in favour of the manufacturers. Two of them come from factory owners, and the third one from a member of Parliament who knew very little about industry first-hand. Sauces A-E on the other hand come from the workers themselves, and thus are much more accurate and reliable.

g) Letters and diaries; newspaper reports; photographs; local record offices.
(364 words.)

7.2 Examiner's comments

There is some curious spelling throughout this answer, but the extracts seem to have been read intelligently and most of the answers are quite sensible. The basic identifications are given in a), but in b) the candidate is mistaken in thinking that both extracts are about child labour – only the first is. The second *may* be, insofar as adult working hours were determined by how long the children could work (many factory owners of this time thought this); but in fact this is not clear from the sources. The first extract is about the benefits to parents and to the poor rates, of child labour; the other is about how effectively a factory can run on shorter hours. That the two are connected needs a much clearer explanation.

In c), the candidate is able to identify the other sources of Britain's greatness quite well, but absolutely fails to grasp the irony in Cobbett's comment. Thus the candidate mistakenly thinks that Cobbett is in favour of juvenile female labour when in fact the extract suggests exactly the opposite. Part d) is quite well answered, though it is worth pointing out that *everyone* working on a loom was in danger from moving machinery, and not just the child crawling beneath the loom. A more qualified answer would help in e): Sources C and J are *not* about the same method of descent, even though both are dangerous. In B the trapper is not sure whether she has light or not, but the boy has light in K. It is making an assumption to state that L confirms the dangers of injury mentioned in C. Fuller development seems to be needed in this answer.

The same is true of f). There should be a clear explanation here of what is meant by *reliability*. To say that something is reliable means that it may be relied on, i.e. that it is actually true. It can, of course, be genuine evidence without actually being true. In fact, none of these pieces of evidence is impartial, and none presents both sides of the case; but they *are* typical examples taken from the period of workers' evidence and the manufacturers' defence, and the cross-sections of opinion which they both represent. The evidence is genuine evidence, though we cannot be sure that the statements made are fully reliable, i.e. true in every case.

As an answer, g) is perhaps rather too skimpy. The ideas should be fleshed out into a paragraph if full justice is to be done to them. 'Letters and diaries' does not seem to be very informative: the answer should make clear *whose* letters and diaries ought to be looked for. 'Local record offices' are a *source* rather than a *type* of evidence; when you have visited the CRO, what exactly are you supposed to be looking for? It is doubtful whether there are any factory photographs before the later part of the nineteenth century, but it is worth mentioning that reports from factory inspectors are available from the mid-1830s, and these contain masses of evidence, most of which seems to be fairly reliable.

This is on the whole another good average answer, but it tends to be too brief and rather lacking in explanation. It will probably miss the highest grades.

UNIT 8 EMIGRATION IN THE NINETEENTH CENTURY

▶ **Assessment objectives 3 and 4: Empathy, and the use of sources**
Word limit: 600 words

Study the sources below, and then answer the questions which follow:

Source A: The English

Thousands are going, and that, too, without mortgaging the poor rates. But sensible fellows! it is not the aged, the halt, the ailing; it is not the paupers that are going; but men with from £200 to £2000 in their pocket! This very year, from two to five millions of pounds sterling will actually be carried from England to the United States . . . From Boston two great barge loads have just gone off to Liverpool, most of them farmers, all carrying some money and some as much as two thousand pounds each. From the North and West Ridings of Yorkshire numerous waggons have gone, carrying people to the canals leading to Liverpool . . . Ten large ships have gone this spring, laden with these fugitives from the fangs of taxation; some bound direct to the ports of the United States . . . There is at Hull one farmer going who is seventy years of age; but who takes out five sons and fifteen hundred pounds. Brave and sensible old man! and good and affectionate father! He is performing a truly parental and sacred duty; and he will die with the blessings of his sons upon his head, for having rescued them from this scene of slavery, misery, cruelty and crime.

(William Cobbett, *Rural Rides*, 1830)

Source B: The Irish

The great mass of the people have small amounts of land with potato patches just large enough to supply them with a few potatoes through the winter . . . These people live in the most wretched clay huts, scarcely good enough for cattle pens . . . They have potatoes enough for thirty weeks of the year, and for the rest, nothing. When the time comes in the spring when this provision reaches its end . . . wife and children go forth to beg. Meanwhile the husband goes in search of work either in Ireland or England, and returns at potato harvest to his family.

(Frederick Engels, *The Condition of the Working Class in England*, 1845)

Source C: The Scots

Every way possible was used to drive the Highlanders away, to force them to exchange their farms and comfortable cottages for the rocks on the seashore. The country was darkened by the smoke of burnings. Many deaths followed from alarm, exhaustion and cold. Some old men took to the roads, wandering around in a state of madness.

(A stonemason, Donald Macleod, writing in 1841)

Source D

On Monday (8 April 1844) one hundred and sixty-five souls, men, women and children, embarked at Deptford, on board the *St Vincent* of 628 tons, preparatory to sailing the following day for Plymouth, where she will receive all who may be assembled there from the western part of England; from thence she will proceed to Cork and take in emigrants from Ireland, quitting the last-mentioned port of 16 April for Sydney . . . The *St Vincent* appears to be a fine vessel, well found, and may the Almighty prosper her voyage, which is usually about four months in duration.

(from the *Illustrated London News*, April 1844)

Source E

Before the emigrant has been a week at sea he is an altered man. Hundreds of poor people huddled together, without light, without air, wallowing in filth and breathing a fetid atmosphere, sick in body, dispirited in heart; the fevered patients lying between the sound . . . their agonized ravings disturbing those around and predisposing them, through the effects of the imagination, to imbibe the contagion; living without food or medicine except as administered by the hand of casual charity; dying without the voice of spiritual consolation and buried in the deep without the rites of the Church. The food is generally ill-selected and seldom sufficiently cooked . . . the supply of water, hardly enough for cooking and drinking does not allow washing. In many ships the filthy beds, teeming with all abomination are never required to be brought on deck and aired.

(Stephen de Vere, in a letter to T.F. Elliott, 1847)

Source F

Fig 5.5
A 'coffin ship' of the nineteenth century, in port (contemporary engraving)

QUESTIONS

a) Are these sources, in your opinion, *primary* or *secondary* historical sources? Give reasons for your answer.
b) What different reasons for emigration are given in Sources A, B and C?
c) How far are the two accounts of emigration given in Sources D and E in agreement with each other? How do you account for the differences?
d) How do you explain the caption to Source F? Which of Sources D and E does it seem more closely to resemble? Give reasons for your answer.
e) Comment on the reliability of each of these sources of historical information. What other sources would a historian wish to examine if he wished to make a study of emigration?
f) If you were a farm labourer whose close workmate was proposing to emigrate to Australia in 1840, how would you set about persuading your wife to accompany you there, and how would you deal with her arguments against the suggestion?

8.1 A student's answer

a) They are all primary historical sources. Though the authors themselves may never have been emigrants, and so cannot be said to have first-hand experience of emigration, all the sources are contemporary sources and are written by people who have a close acquaintance with the subject. Even the artist who drew Source F clearly had a good knowledge of the subject he was portraying.

b) Source A says the emigrants are fit and active people with money in their pockets going to search for a better life, and that they are 'brave and sensible' (thought some are elderly). B says that they arer desperately poor and wretched, and their men-folk are driven to emigrate just so they can send something home for the family to live on. Source C gives us the idea that Scots emigrants are equally as desperate as Irish ones. This may be partly due to the fact that landlordism was as brutal in Scotland as it was in Ireland, and almost as foreign.

c) Sources D and E seem to be agreed on a number of points: the ships were small, the voyage was long, and conditions were generally over-crowded. They also differ to some extent. The ship discussed in Source D seems better than the one in Source E, which is filthy, uncomfortable and hazardous to health. This, however, may have been true to some extent of the first vessel, but since the voyage was still to begin the passengers did not yet know about it. In addition, Source D comes from a published periodical, and may have been putting a good front on things, but Source E is from a confidential letter and may have given a more unvarnished account.

d) Emigration vessels were sometimes called 'coffin ships' because their condition was so unseaworthy as to make them dangerous to human life. They were wooden-built, and if they sank they could easily become the coffin of the people aboard. Such a condition seems to apply more to the ship in Source E than it does to that in Source D, which is said (perhaps truthfully) to be 'a fine vessel.' The ship in Source E, however, is cramped, dark and dirty, with extremely bad food, little water to wash in, and with almost no health or medical provision.

e) Sources A, B and C are all written from first-hand observation and seem to be reliable, especially in the case of C, written by someone who had perhaps experienced the rigours of eviction. The first two, being written by public figures both of whom had an axe to grind, may be somewhat suspect in their sentiments, but there seems to be less reasons why Donald Macleod should lie.

A historian making a study of emigration, however, would need a great deal more information. He would need copies of the advertizing literature published by those organizing emigration, manifests and other documentation from the shipping companies, information from government offices relating to emigration statistics, and possibly further information from the countries to which these people emigrated. For immediate detail he would probably look at personal records, since many people, embarking on something of great importance for the first time in their lives, might try to keep a journal of their experiences to show their children in later life.

f) I should point out to her that rents were high and that we also had to find church tithe and poor rates out of our meagre income, that our living standards were miserably low and that as we got older we were likely to become poorer, with no future in this country except in the parish workhouse. Our lives were hard, we worked twelve or more hours every day, and lived in cottages that were little better than pigstyes. We weren't allowed to hunt or poach, there were still spring traps threatening our life and limb, and we were generally treated like dirt by the landlord's bailiffs.

If my wife objected on grounds of the dangers of the voyage, I should try to reassure her by pointing out that it had been done before, and that it was worth the risk. If she objected that she would lose touch with her family and friends, I should say that we should soon make new friends and have a better life. If she objected to the expense, I should tell her that travelling steerage we could get to America for fifteen pounds and to Australia for less than forty. If our growing children came with us, the work would be little more than it is at the present time.
(646 words)

8.2 Examiner's comments

The answers here are concise and sharply on target, even though the answer as a whole runs on rather longer than the 600 words prescribed. The answers to a) and b) are brief and sensible, the latter quite intelligently picking up (and possibly somewhat over-playing) the idea that some emigrants went to the colonies with the legitimate idea of improving themselves whilst others less fortunate were driven to it as the last act of desperation – the comparison of Scottish with Irish landlords is quite original and shows that the student is thinking about the work.

In c), the central point – that the former is the description of a *ship* at the *outset* of a voyage, whilst the latter is concerned with *passengers* actually *during* the voyage – is clearly made. Source D is particularly vague about the *number* of passengers: 165 for a ship of little more than 600 tons, and with an indeterminate number still to be picked up at Cork – this point could have been noticed and high-lighted. The same is true of the answer to d); the point connecting wooden ships with wooden coffins is well-made, but the reasons for linking the illustration with Source C instead of Source D could have been more tellingly explained.

Part e) is well-handled, though once again, as in Unit 8, more should perhaps have been said about *reliability*. Nevertheless, the student seems to grasp the idea of reliability: the point about public figures writing for propagandist purposes ('with an axe to grind', as the student puts it), and ordinary individuals writing from their own experiences is a telling point to make. The student also hints briefly at another good point – things written in private diaries and journals are more likely to be true than those which are written for publication, where the effect on the reading public has to be taken into account. A brief discussion of reliability, with the comment that 'reliable' = 'true' would have helped here. The second paragraph of this answer contains some good ideas, e.g. on the use of statistics, and literature from shipping companies, but the answer seems rather vague about how this information can be located.

A number of useful points are made in f), though the wife might have put up stronger resistance than she did. She could have indicated her misgivings about leaving home and sailing into unknown lands, about the change in climate, about the arrival of a family and its dependants in a far land without a job or prospects, and so on. Some of the husband's 'answers' to the suggested objections from his wife seem a little glib, and more could have been made of this also, if the wife chose to rebut his arguments. The disruption of family relations in a world of slow and unreliable transport and uncertain postal communication is a point she would have worried at; it is perhaps the major point that could be made against emigration, and she lets go of it very easily. There are elements of 'role-play' in the empathy employed in this answer, but this seems reasonably acceptable in the light of the form the question takes.

On the whole, however, the answers are sharply focused and very concisely written. There is no particular virtue of length for its own sake, and expressing ideas pithily and fluently is one of the qualities which an assessor will wish to reward. It seems likely that an answer of this sort would be placed amongst the higher grades.